And then She was Free

This is a story of a young woman who has risen above past circumstances to a life of meaning, adventure and self-discovery. Her story needed to be told, not only to bring greater healing to herself, but also to bring healing to the many others who are silent about their struggles. Carli's story will help them see that they are not alone and that they can rise up too.

— *Nicola Bartel, Executive Director*
Mercy Ministries of Canada

I am in AWE of Carli's story. Only God can take this ordinary young Canadian girl with her wounds and hurts and transform her into the extraordinary, powerful, compassionate and selfless woman that she is! This is not a movie; this is real life and Carli's commitment to changing Uganda "one child at a time" is not just talk. Carli is Romans 8:28 in action, "And we know that God causes all things to work together for good to those who love God, to those who are called according to His purpose." (NASB) Her story is not over. I am looking forward to financially and prayerfully supporting Carli's kids at Abetavu for years to come as she and Robert continue to do what God has called them to do.

— *Ingrid Janzen, Children's Pastor*
Riverside Community Church

And then She was Free

CARLI TRAVERS

AUTOBIOGRAPHY

AND THEN SHE WAS FREE

This autobiography is based on what the author thought and saw through her experience. The memories of her life are her own. The conversations in this narrative all come from the author's recollections – though they are not written to represent word-for-word transcripts. Rather, the author has retold the dialogues in a way that evokes the feeling and meaning of what was expressed. In all instances, the essence of the dialogue is accurate and all the events are true.

ISBN 978-0-9947489-0-4

DEDICATION: TO MY FELLOW SURVIVORS

You are strong.

You are beautiful.

You are courageous.

Do not allow your past to consume or undermine you.

Do not give up hope.

Freedom is yours for the taking.

Spread your wings and fly.

Foreword

This book commands *"Rise up and take your rightful place"*. The God of Heaven says, "Though your voice was silenced I will make you loudest of all". The One that does not initiate suffering, but always turns it around, ashes to beauty, pain to purpose. He takes our seething self hatred and turns it inside out to a love that dominates our greatest fears and conquers our greatest challenges. This kind of love sets other captives FREE! I predict, one by one as the words in this book penetrate eyes, hearts and souls, this reality will be won by multitudes and the truth will be realized: that it was always past tense and then she was free.

— Carolyn Twietmeyer
Founder and Executive Director of Project HOPEFUL (nfp) and CEO, Walk on Water Inc.

Acknowledgements

To our *Friends of Abetavu*, for continuing to support our work financially. We have come a long way because of the amazing contributions that we have received. Without their help we would have never come this far or have been able to expand our projects. Many lives have been given a sense of hope and a brighter future because of them.

The following are only a few of the other amazing people that have helped me throughout the personal and professional process of enabling me to share this part of my journey.

My husband, *Robert Birungi*, for always believing in me and for his love and support. I could not ask for a better partner to go with me through this adventure that is our life.

My parents, *Ron* and *Carol Travers*, for supporting me as I strive for healing and freedom. Writing this book has been hard for the whole family, but it has also brought us closer together and I thank God for this.

My sister, *Kristin Loveridge*, for supporting me emotionally through numerous back and forth 'Facebook' messages. For encouraging me that this was my story to tell and to not give up. She has always had a strong backbone that I have admired. Even though she is my baby sister, I look up to her.

Elaine Gibson, for sharing her God given gift of counselling. She played a huge role in helping me to discover the hurting little girl inside me and to see the importance of setting her free.

The *Abetavu staff*, for all of their hard work and dedication to bettering the lives of our children and the people of our community.

Michell Holmquist, for planting the seed for the idea of the title for my memoir.

Jacqui Kempton, for standing by me from the very beginning when my memoir was just a dream. When I was struggling emotionally, still feeling dragged down by the control of my abuser, she gave me the proverbial 'kick in the pants' to push forward and to stop doubting myself. She and her husband *Ken Dyck* and daughter *Ashley Kempton* have become a very special part of my life.

Victoria Dix, for word processing my hand written journal manuscript so that I could have a break from the emotional toll that writing had had on me.

Ranjit Samra, for voluntarily sketching the cover. He has also been a great friend, providing encouragement along the way.

Brenda Hewer, for voluntarily providing her amazing expertise in formatting the cover and providing the design and layout of the entire book. Her attention to detail is extraordinary.

Kamal Dhillon and *Cea Sunrise Person*, both brilliant Canadian writers, for inspiring me from the beginning and for also happily providing guidance about writing and publishing.

Janice GT Penner, for voluntarily editing my memoir and being sincerely dedicated to the entire process. Her care and compassion for Abetavu and myself is a Godsend.

Diane Liva, for helping with the final editing during her stay with us in Uganda.

Kris Baker, President of DMI Ministries, for believing in me from the very beginning.

Frank Gish and *Joanna Mereu*, for their beautiful hearts and words of wisdom that helped me keep my focus throughout this book writing journey.

Last, but not least, my beautiful children: *Kingston, Zion, Xavia, Justina, Akiz, Colin, Codrine, Isaiah, Juliana, Annette, Yawe, Sandra, Douglas, Deus, Benjamin, Martin, Ty, Godance, Marjorie, Christine, Barbara* and *Tina*, and my adorable grandson *Jeremiah*. From the bottom of my heart I thank you for blessing me with the most precious gift of being your Mommy and Grandma. Special thanks to the older kids for helping to "referee" your younger siblings so that I could have time to work on this memoir.

"Healing doesn't mean the damage never existed. It means the damage no longer controls your life."

— Akshay Dubey

Introduction

Running.

My mind is infamous for running a million miles a minute, but it would always settle back on a little girl. A little girl with big, piercing blue eyes. Her voice was silent, not one word vocalized. She wanted to speak. In fact, she wanted to shout, but there was a dark presence in the room that forced her mute. I wanted to help this little girl. Her eyes spoke of the pain that her lips could not utter.

I finally forced myself to truly open my eyes to what was before me. My heart beat faster and faster. The dark room enveloped me with a fog of despair. A hand reached through the shadows and touched my body. Fear pierced through my entire being like I was being pricked by thousands of needles. Anger pulsated through my heart. I looked down and was horrified to see that I was naked. I felt disgusted with myself. I looked around but could not see the little girl any more.

That is because the little girl was me. The words that she could not speak because of the threats she received does not scare the woman that I am today. I refuse to let my painful past determine my future.

I am now a strong woman because of my faith, determination and stubbornness. My desire to seek justice and my love for vulnerable children and the oppressed all derives from this.

Breaking free and firmly setting my feet forward, no matter how many times I have been thrown back, is all about my journey. It's a journey that I have embraced even though I am only able to take baby steps sometimes.

There is a joy in freedom that words cannot even begin to describe.

And then she was free.

Chapter 1

Ugandan soil, the red fertile gift from God, is where my heart has learned to beat again. It is here, full of a renewed joy for life, that I have learned to spread my wings and fly. Not that long ago, joy and spreading my wings were things I believed that I did not deserve.

There is no easy way to start this story.

During my early childhood, I was sexually abused by an extended family member.

"Now Carli, this is how I show my love for you. I only do this because you are my favorite," he would say.

I have a vivid memory of one of the attacks. I was staying at his home for a family visit. My younger sister and I shared a bed made with a pull out couch. We were alone in the basement but not for long. In the middle of the night I heard the stairs to the basement creaking. With each heavy footstep my heart echoed in fear. I tried to pretend that I was in a deep sleep but he was not going to be convinced. His disgusting hands reached under the unzipped sleeping bag.

"Carli, this is a golden opportunity. It should not be wasted," he said. I tried to turn away but he pulled me back and forced his hands under my night gown. His actions became more extreme than I could remember them being in the past.

"Stop," I said in a quiet whisper.

"Stop," I repeated a little louder.

"STOP!" I shouted.

He quickly put his hand over my mouth, looking at me sternly as if I was a child that deserved to be scolded. "You see your little sister there? How about I show her our special time instead of you?" he sneered.

"I'm sorry," I cried. As much as I wanted it all to stop, wishing that I could crawl inside myself and disappear, he would have to kill me before he touched my sister. Yet again the coward, the creep, the pedophile, got his personal satisfaction. I lay on the sofa bed feeling disgusted with myself.

"I love you kiddo," he said.

"I hate you," I spat back at him.

Falling to his knees he cried, "I do this to you because I have no choice. If it was not for you, I would have to find another little girl. You have helped me."

With that final plea I became his vice. As much as I hated him and what he did to me, I could not let another little girl carry the burden that weighed me down into the depths of despair.

I saw a counsellor when I was about 12 years of age. During the entire 45 minute drive to her office I fought an inner battle. Was this my chance to be set free? I sat in her chair full of pride. From somewhere very deep within I had found an ounce of courage, just enough to cautiously whisper, "A family member has been touching me and I don't want him to hurt anyone else." I breathed a huge sigh of relief and felt the weight of the world lift off my shoulders. She kindly encouraged me to share more, so I bravely opened up about the entire situation.

"Thank you for sharing. I know this must have been difficult for you. I am going to ask you to wait in the reception area while I talk with your dad," she said. I was so relieved that I would not have to see Dad's reaction. Seeing his pain and feeling that I was the cause would be far too much weight for my newly found wings to bear.

The car ride home was awkward. "So how was the counseling session?" Dad asked too casually. I quickly looked at him trying to read his face, but it did not show any emotion.

"Fine," I answered with a teenager's typical 'go-to' response.

When we got back home I went to bed and that was that. My precious wings had been clipped. My sense of self-worth was gone. I was mortified. Had my parents sided with the abuser over their own daughter? Were my parents too disgusted with me because of what this man had done? These questions haunted me.

Through all of the pain, my faith in God kept me grounded. I was born and raised in a Christian family so going to church every Sunday was a must. I even attended a private Christian school for my secondary schooling, went on missions trips to the Caribbean and Mexico, and attended youth group at the church regularly. My relationship with God was more than these activities; it was intimate. In the depths of my despair He was always there. In God I was never forgotten.

Family holidays were still spent together with relatives, which only enabled my abuser in his claim to innocence. His actions broke me to pieces every time. Years later when I was 17, my father explained that the counselor had never told him anything about the abuse. However, by the time this came to light, I had already buried myself in an extremely unhealthy relationship.

Chapter 2

I contemplated suicide but thankfully never successfully went through with it. I wanted to disappear. I definitely succeeded in this. I lost myself, my complete identity, in a man. From the very beginning I knew he was not right for me. There was no blinding honeymoon phase like the start of most relationships. He was raw and real from the beginning, never minding to hide his temper or the anger that continued to boil up inside of him.

I should have ended things, but I didn't. I believed that this was the hand I had been dealt. I was convinced that the abuse I suffered left me a disgusting piece of garbage, and that I was lucky that I was even able to find a man who would be willing to be with me. At 17, soon after high school graduation, I moved out of my parents' home to live with him. He could not, or chose not to, keep a job or provide a steady income believing that every job was beneath him or not up to his standards. I put myself through school full time as a Community Social Service Worker at Douglas College by working two to three jobs at a time.

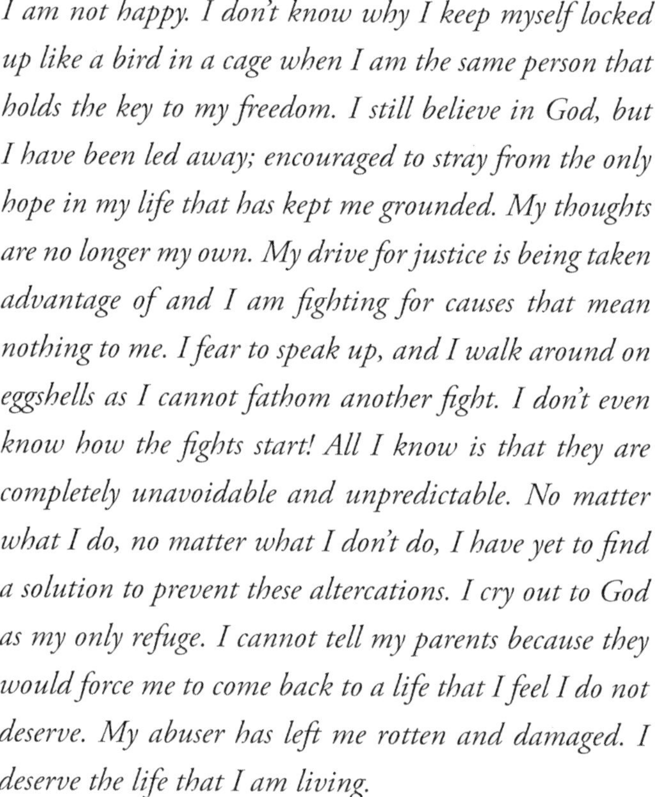

From Carli's Journal

I am not happy. I don't know why I keep myself locked up like a bird in a cage when I am the same person that holds the key to my freedom. I still believe in God, but I have been led away; encouraged to stray from the only hope in my life that has kept me grounded. My thoughts are no longer my own. My drive for justice is being taken advantage of and I am fighting for causes that mean nothing to me. I fear to speak up, and I walk around on eggshells as I cannot fathom another fight. I don't even know how the fights start! All I know is that they are completely unavoidable and unpredictable. No matter what I do, no matter what I don't do, I have yet to find a solution to prevent these altercations. I cry out to God as my only refuge. I cannot tell my parents because they would force me to come back to a life that I feel I do not deserve. My abuser has left me rotten and damaged. I deserve the life that I am living.

Somewhere in the middle of this, I managed to join politics representing the Green Party and ran for MP, MLA and School Board Trustee all before my 21st birthday. Seeking justice is something that has been burning inside of me from a very young age since I was never able to receive it for myself when I needed it. I am still determined to do whatever I can to seek justice for others. Politics and studying social work were my stepping stones to meeting this need.

There were times when the fights at home with the man I lived with were becoming dangerous. His temper and the way he unleashed it towards me continued to break down any bit of self-worth that I was able to gain through my other relationships and activities. As with most people, on the outside it appeared I really had it together, or at least I thought it did. One day, one of the instructors of my program called me to his office. "Carli, we have some concerns that there may be something going on as your marks are deteriorating. We care and we want to help," he said.

This was my out! My heart leapt at the chance to share everything – all of the pain that was rotting within my heart. Instead, I convinced myself that I could not risk my instructors learning about my disgusting past or my unhealthy relationship. I did not want to humiliate myself. I had a chance to leave my pain at the table, to utter the words that were burning deep within me, but I lied. I quickly made up some story and that was that. Walking away, my feet were heavier than ever before. When I got home, I faced a huge fight. As usual everything was somehow my fault. It became too much, so I ran out the door and hid in the shared laundry room of our building.

A usual, my neighbour had heard everything. "Carli, please leave him. You are so young and beautiful and you deserve so much more than this. I was just like you once. Do you want to end up like me, a single mom of two living in a one room suite?" she pleaded.

Here was another caring friend on the same day giving me an out, a chance to break free. God was really reaching out to me, longing to pull me through. Unfortunately, I truly believed that I was not worth anything. Still extremely overwhelmed by the abuse and an overpowering relationship, I accepted both as my fate.

Drying my tears, I walked back up the stairs and opened the door to the only future that I knew I had. I sat next to him on the couch and we started making wedding plans. Eight months later we were married. Most people were not shy to share their disapproval of this union and their comments only echoed the way that I felt. This was all that I believed I deserved and I did not expect anything more. His temper only got worse and the fights were almost a daily occurrence. I became numb, my actions robotic. Little did I know that a miracle was about to take place. My life was about to take a drastic turn. I was about to be given my ticket out – literally.

From Carli's Journal

Today is the day that I have accepted my fate. I was given two 'once in a lifetime' chances today. Two! But instead I simply walked away. Who does that? What was I thinking? Anyway, it is too late now. Actually it was too late a long time ago. I just don't understand myself sometimes. I will fight for anyone, even a stranger, until the finish but for myself I don't even try. I don't even flinch. I don't hate myself, but I also don't love myself. There are very few people that are happy for our relationship. My friends and family are not fools. I try my best to hide my pain and to put on a happy face. I know that no one forced me into this relationship but I also don't know how to walk away.

Chapter 3

If someone had asked me where Uganda, was I am not sure I would have been able to guess that it is in Africa, let alone point it out on a map. The Social Work department of my school organized a pilot project to send four students to Uganda for a three month practicum. I do not even remember what I wrote on the application, or what even gave me the courage to do so, but I submitted it and was accepted. It was a miracle in itself that my husband even allowed me to go. Only 21 years of age and a newlywed of just seven months, I embarked on not only a life changing, but a life saving journey.

I was timid and still broken from a painful past and present, but there was something beginning to change from deep within. As I boarded the plane and fastened my seatbelt, I felt a sense of relief overtake me. I closed my eyes and thanked God for the peace I felt. I heard a clear and firm voice like no other. "Spread your wings and fly. Soar like the eagle you were meant to be." Tears suddenly flowed down my cheeks. My faith, my trust in God, is something that has always kept me strong. God's words of affirmation were tattooed on my heart. I had discovered a new thirst for life and could not wait to get off the plane and test my own wings.

From Carli's Journal

God was that really you? You want me to spread my wings and fly? Me??? How can I fly when I barely even know how to walk for myself? I take steps, even leaps ahead for others, but for myself? This is going to be a challenge. I yearn to fly and even soar and be free. I have no idea at all what lies ahead of me, but I am not afraid. I am overwhelmed by a sense of peace that I have never felt before. My tears keep flowing and the people on the plane are starting to stare, but to be honest I don't even care. My tears are not of sadness but relief. The burden of abuse and this unhealthy relationship is still heavy on my shoulders, but for the first time in my life I feel like it is no longer mine to carry and that one day, maybe just maybe, I will be free. Please God let this be true.

The weather in Uganda was humid. The smell of body odour was overpowering, but at the same time, I did not find it offensive. What was more concerning was the mountain of suitcases, bins and boxes that lay ahead of me. It was as if the plane had just vomited everyone's belongings there on the floor. I followed other people's movements. Those who were obviously veteran travelers were carefully climbing and maneuvering about the chaos. Finally, I found my entire set of luggage. I hauled the suitcases, which easily matched my own weight, over to a trolley.

My colleagues and I travelled to Masaka where we were to be stationed. Fertile plains rolled into each other only to be separated at times by small trading centres scattered along the main road. Everything was a new experience: squatting in a pit latrine, sleeping under a net, hearing different languages and seeing new faces to name a few. Oddly enough I felt at home – as if my whole life was waiting for this moment in time.

For my practicum I was placed in an HIV/Aids clinic. The atmosphere was extremely depressing, especially for the children. Some people walked for miles every month to receive their life saving treatment, but the place still had a feeling of death row. The structure itself was beautiful and had a first world flair to it, but there was no joy within the walls. For wings that wanted to fly, this was a very demotivating environment. I was not going to have it!

The self-worth I myself was trying to gain back was clearly depleted in the women and children around me. Instead of feeling overwhelmed by the haze of despair that enveloped the clinic, I made it my mission to be a friend and show love and compassion. Language was a huge barrier, so I would simply hold a woman's hand while she cried or welcome her and the children with a hug.

"Please Carli, I need to talk with you in my office," my supervisor said with anger resonating in her voice. Starting to panic, I quickly racked my brain. What had I done wrong? "My staff has brought to my attention something that has upset them. Please, you cannot keep hugging the patients. My staff said that our patients are now expecting them to hug them. I am leaving for a trip and won't be back until after you leave, so I hope that we can reach a solution," she shared with deep concern.

"I promise to reduce my hugging," I said with a shy smile while reaching to give her a goodbye hug. This left us giggling like school girls while she walked away shaking her finger at me, part joking, part serious.

From Carli's Journal

Can you imagine??? Of all things! I have been reprimanded by my practicum supervisor for hugging people!! I cannot stop laughing. I did not realize that my hugs would become such an 'injustice.' I realize that the culture here in Uganda can be quite conservative at times, but I never thought that providing a reassuring or consoling hug to a woman or child would be such an offense. Thankfully my practicum supervisor is not really annoyed but instead speaking on behalf of her concerned colleagues. I know the best solution for this! Welcome hugs tomorrow for all of my colleagues as they arrive for the morning staff meeting. Maybe they were feeling left out. Besides, my practicum is coming to an end anyways. It can't hurt to try.

The next day at practicum I ran up the stairs excited for a new day. It had been pouring rain all morning, so the only staff that had reached the clinic was the janitor. I found a grandmother pacing the tiled floor tracking mud with each step. In her arms were filthy rags. Our eyes met. "Madam, baby sick," she cried as she placed the rags in my arms. I sat on the bench and opened the package before me, peeling away one wet muddy cloth at a time. Suddenly, two sullen eyes stared back at me. Here was a fragile, naked baby boy that weighed no more than 5 pounds. His breathing was laboured and his precious little body fought hard for each gasp of air. Once the severity of the situation slapped me in the face, I started trembling.

"Help! Someone! Please help!" I screamed, never looking up, scared that he may slip away in that second. When no one answered, I realized that I was alone with the janitor. Even the grandmother had gone, her muddy footprints being mopped up as if she never even existed. I removed my sweatshirt and swaddled the baby the best I could. I rocked him and prayed and sang to him. For what I wish was a lifetime our eyes locked. "Please don't go. I love you," I pleaded. His lips parted one last time and then he was gone. All within forty minutes he was displaced, abandoned, orphaned and died. I gently kissed his forehead, closed his eyes, and cried for the angel whose name I would never know.

From Carli's Journal

A baby died in my arms today. A precious and innocent life. God, is this what you meant when you said that I would be spreading my wings and flying? I did not even know his name. It is like the whole world forgot him, like he never existed, even before he took his last breath. I prayed and pleaded, but he still slipped away. My heart is so very heavy. I was not prepared for this, but I really don't know how someone would prepare themselves for such a tragedy. I am grieving for a life that I barely even knew. In all of the despair I am thankful that he was not left to die alone. I hope and pray that he felt my love until the moment that he went to heaven. I am overwhelmed by how much I miss and long for this precious one who remains a stranger to me.

Chapter 4

Each morning the sun rose like clock work. Every day it was my prayer to learn to practice my new found independence. I gathered up every bit of courage and broke ties with my husband. When his temper flared as I had expected it to, I stopped all forms of communication and made plans to move back to my parents' home after my time in Uganda.

From Carli's Journal

I can't believe what I have just done. I have broken things off with my husband. I told him everything that had been burning up inside of me. He seemed confused, as if I was delusional, but reality seemed to hit him when I said that I would not be coming back to him. He is very angry with me, but I don't care. Oh, it feels so good to be able to tell him exactly what I want to say and not have to worry about any repercussions. Thank you, God, for giving me the opportunity to break free. It is a miracle in itself that my husband even allowed me to come to Uganda. I am actually starting to feel and believe that I do deserve better, that there is more for me in life. I was not brought this far for nothing. Now it is time to discover my purpose. Baby steps.

Then, for the first time, malaria got a hold of me. My colleagues took amazing care of me. The fevers made me so delirious that I imagined giant cockroaches crawling all over my body. When I was better, we took a trip to Jinja and Kampala. Travelling was always an interesting adventure – except for the overwhelming attention from men.

During my time in Uganda, there was often someone trying to seduce me with unending praise, usually in hopes of obtaining a Canadian visa. At that time in my life I was completely turned off by men and could be quite rude about it. While my colleagues and I were celebrating in Kampala, I was introduced to a Ugandan artist, a painter and rugby player extraordinaire named Robert. He claimed to be selling his artwork to put himself through school, but I would have nothing of it. "I did not come all this way to the big city to get scammed. We are here to have fun and I am not interested in your so-called art that you claim to do," I jeered. He glared hastily at me as I walked off and left him with my friends.

As the night went on a growing entourage of drunken creepy men pursued me. "Robert, go and get Carli," one of my concerned friends pleaded.

He walked over and reached for my hand. "I came to help

you because your friend asked me to," Robert explained.

"I can handle myself, thank you," I lied. He walked back towards my friends to relay the message, mumbling to himself about how annoying white girls can be. Before I knew it, one sweaty bald man did not take 'no' for an answer. From across the crowds of people my eyes met Robert's. He saw the sheer panic on my face, shrugged off the way I had shot down his previous attempt to rescue me, and marched through groups of people like a soldier on a mission and kindly escorted me back to my friends.

It was late and we had to get back to Masaka the next day so we started to say our goodbyes. "My wallet! I lost my wallet!" Robert exclaimed. Honestly, it probably got stolen from his pocket during one of his rescue missions saving the stubborn white girl. For his transport I gave him only 1000 Ugandan shillings, the equivalent of about 40 cents Canadian. It was definitely not one of the most generous moments in my life. Little did I know this so called 'con-man' from Kampala would later become my 'knight in shining armour.'

From Carli's Journal

We had a fun weekend in the big city. I am so blessed to have such a great group of girls to share my Ugandan practicum with. I am the baby of the group and they are always looking out for me with the most genuine intentions. I met a Ugandan guy called Robert on one of the nights that we went out. I am actually quite embarrassed as I was behaving rude and stuck up. I don't know what came over me, as from what I believe, that is not my usual behavior. I think that because I have been hurt by some of the men in my life I am not able to trust and I have been left scarred. Maybe I was trying to exercise my new found independence. Maybe I was trying to prove to myself that I was in charge and could take care of myself. Either way it blew up in my face and the polite man, Robert, kindly persisted through my arrogant stance and gently guided me to safety. To be honest if I was him I would have given up and left me to fend for myself, but he didn't. There is something special about this guy.

My time in Uganda came to an end. For personal reasons I did not want my husband to know of my arrival date in Canada. He kept managing to hack into my e-mail until I was able to find a secure site. Not one to take 'no' for an answer, he refused to accept that I was moving out and that the marriage was over. It was one thing to have the courage to break things off when I was miles away separated by oceans and continents, but going back to face the reality that I would only be a 20 minute drive away was hard to fathom. I could not hide forever and needed to face the consequences of marrying a man who was not meant to be part of my future. After only ten months of marriage, at the tender age of 21, I filed for a divorce with my parents' help.

Everything became so complicated again. I felt like I was adding yet another disgraceful monument to my already checkered past. I hit a new low. My wings and the promise to soar were short lived. The abuse from my past consumed me. Evil lies chained me down into a depression. In my mind, my body was left deformed by the abuse. I felt ugly, unlovable and useless. The stench of my abuser still lurked in the depths of my being. No matter how long I bathed or how hard I scrubbed, I could not make it go away. A failed marriage and a pending divorce only confirmed my innermost belief that nothing good could ever become of me. Fortunately God had different plans.

From Carli's Journal

I am terrified. I am not ready to go back to Canada. I know that I cannot hide forever, but I wish that I could. Any ounce of courage that I had I must have left in Uganda because as the plane gets nearer to my final destination I feel like I am going to have a panic attack and pass out. What have I got myself into? I hate myself enough for what my abuser did to me but now I add the embarrassment of a divorce on top of it. Now everyone will see me for how I have been feeling about myself for so long, a disgusting piece of garbage, a wasted life. I feel like yet again my abuser has triumphed. I was so proud of myself, taking the big step to be free from an unhealthy relationship, but now I am confused and scared. Please God, I want to spread my wings and soar like you promised, but with such burdens weighing me down, how will your promise ever come to pass?

Chapter 5

Not only had my failed marriage brought me a lot of pain, it also brought me a ton of debt. When we were together all of the financial responsibilities had always fallen on my shoulders. Even though my combined pay checks never amounted to more than $1200 a month, I was still left with the burden of rent, electricity, his car payment and insurance, his phone bills, his credit card bills and food. My income barely even scratched the surface, so most of it ended up on my credit cards which continued to accrue interest while I was unemployed and volunteering in Uganda. He even managed to rack up a credit card debt on a card that he had applied for while I was in Uganda. The collectors came after me!

If I was going to get through this, I needed to find a job. Before I knew it I was hired at the daycare in my church. I worked with a young boy with special needs. Every bit of progress the boy made gave me the courage to also start taking baby steps to better my own life. The staff was so loving and accepting of me and truly cared as if we were a family. I would start my shift feeling down, but by the end of each day, they had built me up. I started to realize that they saw something in me.

I had only been back in Canada for one month, but my heart yearned to return to Uganda. I could not shake it from my mind. I ate, slept and breathed Uganda. I really loved my new job but realized this was a God-given stepping stone. It was hard for me to believe that this broken down mess of a young woman still had a bigger purpose. Nonetheless, with the little courage that I had managed to muster up, I took a brave, bold step. On the same date that what was supposed to be our first wedding anniversary, I bought a ticket back to Uganda. I had applied for a divorce, but my husband refused to accept it.

From Carli's Journal 

I have been so blessed by my job, my workmates, and the children in our care. I love going to work each day. The staff is so supportive and caring. The precious boy with special needs that I have been placed with has been such an inspiration to me. At his young age he has gone through so much but he never gives up. How can I allow myself to sulk and sit around feeling sorry for myself when such a positive role model has been placed into my life? God truly sent him to me as an angel. I am slowly discovering my courage. I do my best not to focus on my painful past, but sometimes it's hard. There is still so much pain buried deep within me. I can only hope and

> *pray that one day I will be free. I took a giant leap of faith and booked my ticket back to Uganda. My heart has never been settled since I left. I yearn to go back and I am counting the days until my departure.*

Near Christmas, only weeks before my departure, my husband decided that he was not going to stand for it. "You are my wife and you belong to me and therefore you are not going anywhere. I will not allow it. Do you hear me?" he shouted into the phone adding a mixture of profanity to fully reveal his anger. I was at work on a break and ran sobbing to the bathroom. I couldn't let him take this away from me! I couldn't let this battle for control hang over me anymore!

One of my colleagues found me and I shared my fears. I was so close to ending this toxic relationship, but I was terrified that he had won once again. As much as it pained me to admit it, I knew I was still extremely vulnerable and the chances of his strong grip pulling me back down with him were high. "Carli, you are so close. I have watched you grow and blossom in the past five months. You may not see it yourself, but you are already there. I know that God has huge plans for you. You will get on that plane," she assured me. Her words were firm with a passion that truly wanted to see me succeed. When she hugged me, it was as if it was God Himself. This pep talk saved me from my vulnerability.

I never spoke on the phone or answered an e-mail from that man ever again.

From Carli's Journal

Today started off horribly. It is bad enough that my divorce is still pending, but for my husband to come up with the idea that I was somehow his 'property' and convince me that he had the power to keep me from leaving the country has terrified me. In that very moment I felt so defeated, like all the air had been sucked out of me. Thankfully my co-worker found me sobbing and spoke words that filled up my heart with hope and determination. My marriage will have to come to an end sooner or later whether he likes it or not. I called my lawyer and she said that my husband was just trying to mess with my head and that those were just empty threats. I will never let him intimidate me like this again!

During my family church's annual Christmas dinner, Pastor Kris Baker surprised me with an immeasurable gift. He invited the entire church to financially support my trip back to Uganda. I also teamed up with his registered charity, DMI Ministries, so that I could be under the umbrella of his ministry. He firmly believed in me and the future God had for me before I even touched down in Uganda.

Christmas Day was just around the corner and I was to fly out on the 26th. I may have broken free from my marriage but my abuser still had much control over me. As with any holiday, it was again spent with the entire family. I still saw my abuser, so he was very much part of my life. I was now an adult and no one forced me to attend family events, but at the same time, none of my other family members had yet appeared to stand up against the injustice. I had a dilemma. If I did not attend, everyone would be shocked and confused as to why I skipped out. Even though the white elephant in the room, the pedophile, was on the loose, no one blinked an eye. Instead, we sat around eating a Christmas buffet, sharing pleasantries and making awkward conversation. I felt like the tension in the air was so stiff that a pick axe couldn't have dented the surface, but for our family this was our 'normal.' I never had the courage to stand up against my abuser because the extended family adults that I trusted, those who were supposed to have my best interest at heart, seemed to find it easier for themselves and the 'family unit' if it was just swept under the rug because that would be less painful. So that others could be happy, I had always walked around on eggshells that actually felt like nails at times. This was not a hard concept for me to accept. Leaving meant that I could avoid these painful reminders that my abuser seemingly had more support than I did. Every family get-together felt as if he was winning back innocence; as if I was supposed to pretend that his filthy hands had never violated my body.

These feelings of helplessness had to stop! Boarding the plane back to Uganda was a major step.

From Carli's Journal

I hate seeing my abuser. I absolutely hate it! The mere sight of his hands makes my skin crawl. As soon as I see him, I lose myself and become the terrified little girl that is hiding inside of me. The smell of hot-cross buns baking or seeing some of his furniture like the grandfather clock set off a trigger deep within me. Hearing someone sing "You are my sunshine" is like nails on a chalkboard for me. I keep allowing myself to attend family functions because I don't want to rock the boat. I keep waiting for someone to come to my rescue and stand up and say that this isn't right, but it never happens. I hate how much control he still has over my life; to the point that at times I even pity him. He has a bad heart and is aging; I get scared that if I make a scene, he could become ill. I hate myself for being more concerned about his well-being than mine. I long to break free from these chains. Enough is enough. Please God, let Uganda be the start to my freedom.

Even though I was anxious to break free from those who had hurt me, this also meant leaving behind those that I loved dearly. My precious maternal Grandmother, Nana, truly had a heart of gold. She had overcome so many obstacles in her life, but she was never bitter. Instead, she wore a crown of compassion and spent every single night praying for everyone – even my friends that I had drifted apart from over the years. Her strength and words of wisdom inspired me. She always believed in me. I was also leaving behind my dear maternal Granddad who loved me with a pure genuine love. He was a true gentleman. As a war veteran, he was extremely disciplined and would not put up with any nonsense. He said that he would kill anyone who ever hurt me, so I never told him about the abuse. I was afraid that he would kill my abuser and end up in jail. It was so unfair! I was the victim, yet I had taken on this heavy responsibility of protecting the violator.

Since Nana and Granddad were in their eighties and their health was weakening, I was terrified that this would be my final goodbye. I was also leaving my sister just as our relationship was getting closer. I felt like I was abandoning her, but as usual she was the strong one while I embarked on what would be a journey of a lifetime. I know that deep down inside she wanted to see me free from all the pain, so she selflessly let me go. My parents also believed that this was what was best for me. Without looking back, I jumped onto the plane. It was my first time flying solo. I could not rewrite my past, but I knew that what lay before me held endless possibilities. God was not done with me and this was only the beginning. Uganda was embedded into my heart for a reason.

From Carli's Journal

I cannot believe that I am actually doing this. I am terrified but at the same time excited. Here I am back on a plane that is bound for Uganda. It was not easy to say goodbye to Nana and Granddad. I can only hope and pray that I will see them again. I feel like I have been given a fresh start to my life. I cannot deny my past even if I wanted to as it still bears down on me like a truckload of bricks, but it does not mean that I have to give up. As the plane continues soaring in the sky I am reminded of God's promise to me the last time I ventured to Uganda: I would also spread my wings and even one day I would soar like an eagle. With the burden and pain that I carry, it is still hard for me to believe that this could even be a possibility for my life. Yet at the same time, I refuse to let go of the message that was tattooed on my heart.

Chapter 6

Six children. Six beautiful children changed my life in an instant. I was a mere 22 years of age and only two months into my second Ugandan adventure, but in the blink of an eye I became a mother. To be honest, I had never thought about having kids. I absolutely adored children but if anything, I had only considered the possibility of adopting a boy. With my abuser still very much part of my life, I had made a vow that I would never have a daughter because of the risk of him continuing his revolting cycle of abuse. This was different though. The tables had turned in my favour. For once I was in control. He would never be able to touch one of my precious children. We were safe in Uganda; safe from his disastrous reach.

Street life is no place for an adult, let alone a child. I continued to come across the same group of children huddled outside of a small grocery shop that I frequently visited. Safety and security were essential for the precious young ones that stood before me. I could not fathom continuing to see them confused, lost and consumed by life on the streets anymore. I refused to be like everyone else and just walk by pitying them. I knew from the first time I saw them that we would be a family. God placed all six of them into my heart – an immeasurable blessing. I took them to the Child Protection Services office. “You are a crazy *mzungu* (white person). What do you want with these children?” an officer said glaring at me confusedly. He saw before him dirty burdens with swollen tummies, ring worm and rags for clothes. I saw six angels that yearned for love and family and a place to call home. I worked closely with Child Protection Services to research their backgrounds and each of them was fully assessed and counselled. Each of their stories was horrific. I cried as their painful stories of rape, severe physical abuse, attempted murder, sale to a stranger, and extreme neglect were translated to me.

From Carli's Journal

I could not keep walking by these precious children and continue to do nothing. I am barely settled in myself, still figuring out my life in Uganda as a foreigner. On my better days I still feel and probably look like a deer caught in headlights. I still cannot even cross the street by myself, fearing the hectic traffic that appears to follow no laws. I grab onto any stranger's arm that is nearest to me, close my eyes and say a quick prayer for my life. Anyway I could not give up on these children. I am probably crazy for taking on such a heavy responsibility but being crazy is not always a bad thing. To be honest I am not even sure where to start, but at the same time it all feels so right. I think this is what people mean when they talk about a 'blessing in disguise.'

The youngest was one and the oldest was ten. They had suffered tragedies that most people would not even endure in a lifetime. With the necessary paperwork in my hands, my life changed forever. I was honoured with the title of 'Mother', a lifelong gift that many women take for granted. In the beauty of it all, I had no idea what I had gotten myself into. Thankfully God hadn't planned for me to do this alone.

The 'knight in shining armour' that had come to my rescue during my first time in Uganda had come to my rescue permanently. After I had returned to Canada, our relationship had blossomed over numerous phone calls. I felt safe with him. He never judged me, so I was very open with him about my past and present struggles. When I arrived back in Uganda, we started dating. I fell in love with his heart for children and his courageous strength. As a national star rugby player at the time, he had a tough exterior, but on the inside he was full of compassion for those in need. His creativity and intricate thought shone through his paintings. Robert could have run away and never looked back when I brought forward my intentions of becoming a mother to six children. To be honest, I would not have been surprised. It is rare for an African man to care for non-blood related children. Even in-country adoption is still a very new concept. As you'll see, Robert is not just any man! A survivor of his own rough childhood, he believed the vicious cycle needed to be stopped. Abandoned children needed a family to thrive and be able to contribute back to society. We would be that family.

From Carli's Journal

I never believed that there was a 'knight in shining armour' out there for me. I was prepared to be on my own without a special companion, but God thankfully has different plans for my life. Robert is more than I could have prayed and hoped for. Just today he was easily teaching the kids to draw and paint in our compound. He encouraged each of them and the pride that shone from each child took my breath away. His compassion and care for all of our children comes naturally to him. I am so much in love with this man. He has never judged me for my past and encourages me to move forward. I am so thankful for his love and care. I am excited for what our future holds.

With funds that my parents raised, we were able to rent a house, buy furniture, clothing, and food and enroll the kids in school. Once we were all settled, the honeymoon phase of our new family life ended in about 10 minutes! I don't know why I had assumed any differently, but when you're led by the heart you believe that anything is possible. "Mommy, blah, blah, blah," one of my children shouted as he ran into the sitting room. Okay, "blah, blah, blah" was not exactly what they were saying, but that made no difference. They did not speak a word of English nor did I speak much of their native language, Luganda. Robert was at the market and the awkward silence waiting for my reply felt like hours. Believe me, there is only so much that hand gestures, miming and ridiculous acts of charades can communicate! Even more, a parent really needs to understand when kids are fighting. In the meantime, loving actions filled the void. We bonded as we spent precious time together playing games, hugging, and laughing – mostly at me!

From the very beginning our kids were told that they could call me 'Auntie' but it never stuck. They yearned for a family and decided to bless me with the honour of being their 'Mommy.' It was a heavy responsibility, but it was not burdensome. It was a big life change indeed, but one that I believe from the bottom of my heart, my whole life had prepared me for.

Due to the sexual abuse one of our children went through, she suffered from frequent night terrors. "Get off me!" she would shout. Gently I would bring her back to our bed where she would almost always end up wetting herself, still shaking in terror. Seeing a child go through this and not being able to calm her down is heart wrenching. It often hit a nerve with me and brought back painful flashbacks from the abuse in my past.

From Carli's Journal

One of the children has been suffering with serious night terrors. Even just last night she started screaming at the top of her lungs. I got up quickly to try and calm her down but the way she was trembling broke my heart. It is one thing that I suffered from sexual abuse myself, but to see someone else struggling with it is really devastating. I hope and pray that she will be able to move past this. I don't want her pain to determine her future and I am starting to see that I should not desire any less for myself.

Not wanting to be overcome by this, I would lay awake pleading for God to free us. I could empathize with these children. I never wanted to see any of my children carry the burden that I was still battling with after so many years. I knew they could have a bright future just like I was beginning to have for myself.

The foundation for Abetavu, which means "a safe haven for those in need," was set. A feeling of peace enveloped my entire being. For the first time in my life I felt I had a purpose. The promise God instilled in me at the beginning of that first flight to Uganda had come to pass. My wings were stretched out and I was ready to soar.

Chapter 7

It was a scorching hot day. I was not well. Robert and I walked the dusty road towards the taxis. The drivers were all shouting for us to board, competing for their necessary quota of customers. As usual I ignored the chaos and followed Robert into the taxi of his choice. He was very friendly to everyone and this was helpful as we always seemed to get the best seats. None of this mattered to me at the time since I was overwhelmed with the urgency to vomit. I convinced myself over and over again to do otherwise and only by God's grace did I make the long, hot journey to the clinic.

I was relieved to find the clinic pleasantly quiet, but if I had known my diagnosis, I would have preferred the delay of the usually crowded waiting room! "Travers? Where is Travers?" a nurse asked, stumbling into the waiting room. Slowly standing up, I followed her white, crisp uniform to a room at the end of the hall. Behind the desk sat a familiar face. I had been in his office just a few weeks before.

"Good morning, Madam. Please have a seat. What has

brought you back?" he asked inquisitively.

"The same reason as before," I quickly answered. After scribbling on his notepad, he sent me back down the hall for some blood work and a urine sample. Twenty minutes later I impatiently sat waiting for the doctor to interpret the results from the lab.

"Everything is perfectly fine my dear. The tests show nothing is wrong," he chirped in a sing song voice.

"Then what could be wrong with me?" I demanded.

"Nothing is wrong Ms. Travers. Instead you are pregnant," he said.

The words echoed through my entire being. I was in shock. Somehow I brought myself back to Robert waiting in the reception area. Sinking down into the chair next to him, I shared the news. Ever so gently he took my hand into his and whispered in my ear, "It's going to be okay."

From Carli's Journal

I am pregnant!?!? I still feel like if I pinch myself I will wake up from this dream. Honestly, I am most concerned with how my parents are going to react. First of all, I am not married to the father of my child and secondly, they do not even know him. I feel like I have been enough of a disappointment and don't want to hurt them but

> *I also feel an overwhelming responsibility to protect the precious life inside of me. I know that they will not put any blame on the child, but it will still take me some time to gain the courage to even make the phone call. I am so thankful for the amazing man that I have standing by me.*

Still in the denial phase, I demanded that we go for a second opinion. We went for an ultra sound scan and there was our precious child. As soon as I heard his little heartbeat, there was no escaping the truth. I was already 14 weeks into the pregnancy, past my first trimester, and utterly terrified. I was separated but legally still married, and my 'husband' had no intentions whatsoever of agreeing to a divorce. I had an amazing boyfriend and I was pregnant with his child.

To add to the chaos I was already a mother to six children between the ages of one and ten. All of this came to pass a mere three months after my feet hit Ugandan soil. They had literally hit the ground running!

Telling my parents about the out of wedlock pregnancy was inconceivable. It ate me up alive. I wanted so badly to tell them but I was terrified. Robert and I also wished that we had been married first, but our baby was innocent to our choices. Finally, when the pregnancy reached five months, I knew that it was not right to keep the secret any longer. I mustered up the courage and told my mom over the phone.

To say the least, my parents were not pleased with me and were quite apprehensive about the father of my child, a man that was a stranger to them. Once they were able to get over the shock and their anger settled, their love for the future soccer player kicking away in my womb shone through.

This was a year full of many firsts and precious memories for our entire family. Not only was this my first pregnancy but our kids also had 'firsts' too – first birthday parties and first days at school, ever! The more practical everyday life ones included first time sleeping in a bed, first time using a flush toilet, and the first time having clean running water. Most importantly, all of us were experiencing everything together that year as a first time family.

With the baby's due date quickly approaching, I eagerly yearned for the divorce to be finalized. Robert and I had something special from the beginning. As cliché as it sounds, we know that we were truly meant to be together. We really wanted to get married, but with the divorce pending and my then husband refusing to show up at court, things did not look promising. Finally, after a month long wait, a Canadian judge was able to grant the divorce and we were given the go-ahead to get married. Heavily pregnant, I walked up the six never-ending flights of stairs with Robert. In front of the Justice of the Peace and our witnesses I happily said "I do." All that mattered to me was standing hand in hand with the love of my life, my best friend, committing ourselves to each other before God.

While celebrating our marriage with friends, I held the certificate gently in my hands. When I glanced over it, I started laughing hysterically. Deeply curious, everyone read over the marriage certificate also hoping to join in on this rib-cracking joke. But no one found anything humorous! The bold font date at the top of the certificate was what had me giggling like a little girl. October 31st. It was Hallowe'en day! I could imagine my friends back in Canada picturing a Hallowe'en obsessed gothic themed wedding. On the upside, I knew I would never forget our anniversary!

From Carli's Journal 

Today I married my best friend. I swear that I had to climb up a million steps just to get to the office where we would legally be wed. Being as heavily pregnant as I am the chances of going into labour while we said our 'I do's' did not seem that unlikely. Thankfully baby did not make its appearance and once I caught my breath we went ahead with our civil ceremony. It was simple but perfect. I don't know if it was because of the excitement but it completely did not connect in my brain that today is Hallowe'en. Thankfully, it's not celebrated here so no one on this side of the world has taken any notice. Either way, I am so happy today and for the life ahead of us as husband and wife.

Two weeks later on a very stormy day, our son Isaiah made his debut – although his father is the one who deserved a standing ovation. No matter how many expectant mother books I read from cover to cover, I was not prepared for what was to come. The pain was excruciating, but the midwives only offered me black tea. They believed it helps with the contractions, but it was not for me. When I refused the tea, they unfortunately took it personally. "Tell your wife to stop pushing. Her doctor is stuck in a traffic jam. She needs to be patient," the midwife directed my husband as she walked out the door.

We were left alone in the delivery room. It seems that Isaiah did not get the memo. Without any control, nature took over and my body started pushing. Robert ran to get the midwife, but she just repeated that I must wait. When he came back into the room, he found baby Isaiah was already crowning. The pain was unbearable, but there was no turning back. Robert supported my legs and encouraged me while I pushed our baby into his waiting hands. Robert wrapped baby Isaiah in a clean cloth then tied and cut the cord as if he had been training for this moment his whole life. Seconds later my doctor came running into the delivery room. To her surprise, she found two exhausted parents and a beautiful, healthy baby boy. She could not believe how well Robert had handled the delivery and jokingly offered him a job. The midwives were scolded but remained un-phased. All that mattered to us was that our baby was fine. We thanked God for bringing our precious son safely into the world even though it may not have gone according to plan. That did not matter.

From Carli's Journal

Yesterday I gave birth to a precious baby boy, Isaiah. He is beautiful with a golden complexion and full head of dark, wavy hair. He looks just like his 'Daddy.' I never could have imagined that Robert would have to play such a leading role in our baby's delivery. The way that he kept his cool while I cried and screamed with no doctor in sight was amazing. Considering everything, I thank God that our baby was born without any complications. I am so thankful for this amazing little life in front of me. I can't wait to leave the hospital and bring him home to meet all of his brothers and sisters.

I was now a mother of seven and a newlywed. A new chapter had begun just two days before my 23rd birthday. Just one year before this, I had been ready to give up and succumb to what I believed was all that I deserved – a life of misery and despair.

Chapter 8

"Nana is not doing well and we would like you to come for a visit," Mom informed me over the phone. It's the call that every ex-pat dreads.

Baby Isaiah was just five weeks old and I was very nervous about travelling alone with him. There was not enough time to apply for a Canadian visa for Robert, so there was no other option. I knew in my heart that I had to say good-bye to my mother's mother, my precious 'Nana.' It would also be a chance to visit with my family and friends. I embarked on a journey back to my Canadian roots.

When I stepped out of the airport doors, the cold air burned my insides. The first thing that was on my mind was that I just had to have a 'two cheeseburger meal with a root beer'. This was not a burdensome request since there was a location almost every second block on the way to my childhood home. After filling up on what most people these days refuse to acknowledge as food, I was pleasantly satisfied. Even though I arrived in the evening and was absolutely exhausted, I had to see Nana. She was being cared for in a beautiful hospice which had Christmas decorations adorning the hallway and family room.

With baby Isaiah in my arms, I walked into Nana's room and my heart sank deeply. I hoped that I had entered the wrong room, but there was no denying it. Granddad was gently clasping the fragile hand of a mere shadow of a woman. I could not believe how much she had changed in a year. Nana had been a real 'sweet lover' so she had always been on the larger side. Her fridge was never without a cake, chocolate bars, chocolates, ice cream and many other delightful goodies. She was a proper English hostess and even if one refused her offer, there was no leaving her sitting room without having a proper cup of tea and indulging in a hearty piece of cake. The chocolate bars were usually given as a parting gift. Since she and Granddad lived in the basement suite of my family home, it is a God-given miracle that I never suffered from childhood obesity.

This woman before me was now so fragile and frail. I sat next to her on the bed and placed baby Isaiah in her arms. "My little red pearl," she whispered, her words shaky and hushed. I had no idea what she was trying to say, but I knew in my heart that she knew who we were and how much I loved her.

I could not wait for Granddad's greeting and tender kiss on my cheek. Grandad only knew that I had been in Uganda and that my divorce had gone through. Just before my arrival, my Dad updated him on my marriage and the arrival of his first great-grandchild. This was not an easy task for my father because he didn't know how Granddad would react. "This is the best news that I have heard all year," he had happily chirped back to my dad. He warmly embraced baby Isaiah, his eyes gazing deeply into his. The joy and pride in his face lifted the cloud of despair that was looming in my heart. It was a tragedy to see dear Nana in such poor health, but one thing she was always good at was keeping the family connected and bringing everyone together. Even as her time was soon ending and her words were few, she still managed to reunite her family.

From Carli's Journal

My beautiful 'Nana' is a mere shadow of the woman that I said goodbye to just one year ago. She is so frail and delicate. She can talk, but still her words don't make much sense to me. Her blue eyes speak to me and I could feel them looking deep into my heart. She knows who I am and that means so much to me. I am not ready to let her go or to say good-bye. I love Nana so very much. She is an overcomer and a fighter; so very compassionate and kind to those in need. Even though I now live far away in Uganda, I still need her in my life. It is so painful to watch her slip away.

This was a family that I felt safe with and loved. Nana and Granddad never knew about the sexual abuse that was inflicted on me from the other side of the family. Such news would be too horrific for them at their elderly age, and I did not want anything to take away from the beautiful relationship that we had.

During my short visit I managed to connect and spend time with friends, my sister and other family. I was surprised with a baby shower hosted by Mom and ladies from my home church. Baby Isaiah was generously spoiled. Even though my time was limited, my abuser managed to have the pleasure of my attendance at a family event. Everyone was excited to see baby Isaiah. As I was the first of all my cousins to have a baby, I felt obliged to attend. It was the Christmas season and I did not want to spoil the family get-together.

When you have a sexual predator in the family and the adults are all aware but still find it perfectly fine to celebrate together, or at least pretend to, it is hard for the victim. I was still scared to rock the boat and I lacked the courage to do so even if I wanted to. The freedom that I had worked so hard to gain back was quickly vanishing again. I felt as if my wings had been snapped. It had become a fight for control and in my eyes he had achieved a triumphant victory. I left yet another family get-together feeling ashamed and utterly disgusted with myself. When I got back to my parents' home, I soaked in a scalding hot bath for what seemed like hours, but the filth that engulfed me was much deeper than I realized. The pain was rotting me from the inside out.

From Carli's Journal

I feel so disgusted with myself. Yet again I faced my abuser. I yearn for the courage to say "Enough is enough," and to refuse to attend a family function. Why does he still have so much control over me? I hate this vicious cycle that I allow myself to go through. I tried my best to plaster on a polite smile for everyone, but on the inside I was choking back the urge to vomit. How does everyone just sit around and catch up while my abuser walks around the room taking pictures of a family that he does not even deserve to be a part of? He claims that he respects my personal boundaries by first asking me for permission to hug me. He strategically makes sure that he asks in front of someone who probably knows nothing about the abuse, so I feel like I have no choice. He hugged me and all I wanted to do was scream at the top of my lungs for him to get off of me, to stop touching me with his filthy hands. Now I am left covered in his filth. I bathed and tried to scrub off every part of him, but it did not work. I am lying in bed reliving every memory about him and what he did to me in the past. Please God, I want to break free from these chains. I can't continue to live my life where the abuse and my abuser have control. I want my life back.

Waking up to a new day, I pushed the pain back inside to the corner of my heart that it knew all too well. Nana's health was quickly deteriorating. Every second spent with her was precious. During this difficult time, Dad was able to connect with his old friend who happened to be the editor of a well-known newspaper. Dad told him about my life in Uganda and since it was still the Christmas season, his friend thought my story might be well received as a heartfelt 'soft' news item. There were no guarantees that the story would make the paper, but it was definitely worth a try.

It was near the end of my visit to Canada and I wanted to get my hair cut before I left. It is not the easiest task to find a hairdresser in Uganda that specializes in 'foreign' hair. I found a salon within walking distance from the hospice where Nana was. I left baby Isaiah with my family while they visited with Nana. Just before my hair was about to be blow dried, I saw Dad's reflection in the mirror. "Carli, they put your story in the newspaper. You made the front page! You have already received hundreds of e-mails," Dad said grinning from ear to ear.

As I studied his reflection closer, his smile could not hide his red, swollen eyes. Too scared to turn around and hear the truth face-to-face, I spoke to the man in the mirror. "Nana has died, hasn't she?" I asked solemnly. He nodded back. I do not even know how my legs carried my trembling body back to the hospice. Seeing her lifeless silhouette stirred up a whirlwind of pain. Seeing Granddad sitting in the chair next to her bed holding her hand and sobbing uncontrollably left me gasping for air. My strong British Marine. My WWII war veteran Granddad, whom I had only ever witnessed cry on Remembrance Day, was completely broken. He had truly lost a big part of himself that could never be replaced.

From Carli's Journal

My dear, sweet 'Nana' passed away today. Seeing her lying lifeless was hard enough but seeing Granddad break down and cry shattered my heart into a million pieces. They are both so dear to my heart. My life would have never been the same without them. The only thing that keeps me strong is knowing that she is now looking down on me from heaven and that one day, one very special day, we will meet again.

As hard as the day had been, the article in the newspaper was a blessing beyond measure. Despite some unpleasant e-mails from people judging me and claiming that I was too young to be throwing my life away, a magnitude of financial support and kind messages poured in. Some of these people have since become great friends of ours and have even come to spend time with our family in Uganda.

An intimate funeral was held for my dear 'Nana.' I already missed her tremendously, but I was thankful that I got to say goodbye before my flight back to Uganda.

It was time for me and baby Isaiah to venture back on our long journey home. "You take care of yourself my love. I'm gonna miss you," Granddad said lovingly as he kissed me on my cheek. Sadly, this would be the last time he kissed my cheek – a gesture I treasure greatly.

Chapter 9

Back home in Uganda, our family continued to expand. In three years we went from seven children to 19 and to top it off, I was pregnant with the 20th. Life never threw us a dull moment. Language was no longer a barrier, but a house full of different types of characters, behaviors and struggles was a challenge at times. As a parent who hopes for the best for her children, it was painful to see some of them still driven by the desire to steal, cheat and lie excessively. I could have given up on them and made the all too common mistake of simply justifying their negative issues and behaviors to their painful pasts. This would have been the easy way out, but I was a survivor myself and I refused to allow my past to label me and determine my future. Why would I accept anything less for my own children? 'Giving hope for a brighter future' has been our family motto – something we have done our best to instill in our children.

Unfortunately, school work has been a weakness for most of our kids. Many had never attended a day of class in their entire lives, so the school system was not always very accepting of them. "Mommy, I have brought my brother home. He has refused to stay at school," one of our children shouted as he ran back out the gate towards school. It was only coming to lunch time and when I looked into the face of my child that stayed behind, he refused to make eye contact. We had been struggling to help this boy with his self-esteem, so the look of shame on his face was all too familiar.

"What happened?" I pleaded while taking his hand in mine. After what seemed like hours of silence, he finally revealed an atrocity.

"Mommy, during break time I was teasing one of the girls and I took her popcorn. I did not eat any! I swear Mommy. But she already reported me to a teacher. The teacher hates me. He took me in front of the girl's class and told them to undress me. I was left in my underpants. Then I was brought to my class where the teacher told my classmates to put firewood around me and two of the kids were sent to bring burning charcoals to light me on fire. My teacher said that I am a thief and that this is what happens to thieves. I'm sorry Mommy. I swear. I put the popcorn back. Please, I don't want to die!" he narrated as if he was retelling a bad dream.

I do not even remember how we got to his school so quickly. I think it had something to do with the superhero-like strength that mothers get when their child is in danger. Thankfully, my cousin was visiting at the time, so I had her personal support. In the school office though it only worked against our case. To them, we were just two white women who did not beat children. Therefore, we could never understand their ways of 'discipline' since we were much too 'soft.' The teacher that undressed my child was called into the office. To our surprise, he proudly admitted to every single detail. Even my child's own class teacher, who had encouraged the children to burn him at the stake, was proudly smiling and commending herself for her actions. She repeatedly spat out how stupid she thought my child was. She was well aware that he was sitting next to me with his head down and his tears silently dropping onto the cracked cement floor. This meeting only made things worse. We sat outside the Head Master's office refusing to accept such an outcome. With no hope of any justice for my child, I told him to go and get his backpack from the classroom and that we were going home.

As I was waiting, I heard a commotion from behind the office. "You are just a stupid, dirty street kid and that is all you will ever be!" the teacher shouted while pinching my son's ear. I do not know whose heart those evil words pierced more deeply, but the pain was excruciating.

"If you ever, and I mean ever, touch my child again, I will kill you!" I screamed from a place inside me that I did not even know existed. Angered at my negligence to behave like a proper, respectful Ugandan woman, the teacher intended to slap me, but my reflexes were fortunately quicker and I pushed him to the ground. It was not my finest moment!

I do not condone violence, but this 'Mommy' was not going to stay silent while her son was being ripped to shreds. I take it very personally whenever anyone harms any of my children. As much as I yearned for it, no one had ever shouted or snapped at my abuser. At least I had never witnessed it. I never saw him reprimanded and this only fed my belief that my abuser had full control. I needed each of my children to know that through the good, the bad, and the ugly, we were in this together as a family. Being in our family meant being protected.

From Carli's Journal 

Today one of our children was brutally bullied by the teachers of his school. They even threatened to kill him by burning him with fire. Of course they claimed that they were just joking, but I find nothing whatsoever funny about it. I rushed to the school quickly with my cousin Brianne but we were shocked by the response! It was devastating to see our son experience this. My heart breaks for him. The teachers were laughing and ridiculing him as if he was not even in the room. They were humiliating him, belittling him and because of this, I lost full control over my actions and attacked the male teacher. To be honest, I felt much better after our confrontation. I never condone violence for violence but you also don't mess with any of my children no matter who you are. I am not too sure what tomorrow holds for his schooling, but most importantly I am going to do my best to make sure that he feels loved, safe and secure.

Togetherness is the thread that entwines our family as one. A biological or non-biological tie holds no value in our home. When a new child is brought into the family there is often no more than an hour's notice and it usually happens while most of our kids are at school. No matter the details, a beautiful connection always transpires. Without any direction our kids jump right in. The older ones set up a bed and give a tour of the house. Whoever is closest in size shares some clothes until new clothes can be bought. The young ones, who are full of love and curiosity, climb all over their new sibling. It is amazing how well children can adapt to a new environment when they feel secure and loved. Our kids, young and old, play a huge role in helping our newest family members settle in. We are so blessed to be able to witness their compassion and beautiful hearts at work. By blessing me with the honor of being their mother, they also brought me in as their family and gave me the courage to want and believe in more for myself. They have also been a major part of repairing my broken wings and urging me to soar.

Chapter 10

"Mommy, there is a lady who wants to see you!" one of my kids shouted from outside in the compound. Baby Xavia was just 2 weeks old and we were napping in my room. Half asleep, I left baby Xavia in bed and slowly got up and walked outside. My first glance of the lady was that she was not familiar to our family, however I noticed right away the young child in her arms – it was our son Isaiah! As I got closer to her, she quickly glanced at me as my child screamed in her arms. I sucked up the pain from my recent caesarean and ran towards them. Thankfully, Isaiah was putting up enough of a fight that he slowed her down. By the grace of God, I was able to slam the small door in the gate and lock it before she could leave our compound.

"Where are you taking my son?" I demanded.

She refused to answer. Instead she scowled at me as if I was the one in the wrong. Isaiah was sobbing uncontrollably, reaching towards me with all his might. Her grip on his trembling body tightened with every movement he made.

Using full force, I was able to pry Isaiah out of her clenched fingers. In a blink of an eye she thrust out a knife.

"You stupid *mzungu*. This was not supposed to be like this! Just give me the child and everything will be fine!" she demanded like a soldier sent out on a mission.

I shouted for the older kids to come and I quickly threw Isaiah into their arms. As they ran back to the house for safety, the woman pounced on me like a wild cat-scratching, biting and waving her knife in the air. With all my might, I threw my body on top of her and pushed the hand with the knife firmly against the rough cement. I implored the kids to scream for help at the top of their lungs and one of them bravely came and stepped on the knife that was pressed flat against the ground.

Soon people came to our rescue, bound her arms and legs, and took her to the police. I ran back into our home and found that Isaiah had cried himself to sleep and was nestled in my bed next to baby Xavia. I curled into bed as close as I could get and swore to never let go. Once I got settled, my body started to reveal the physical pain that I was in. Upon a quick inspection, I discovered that my arms and torso were covered in bruises, scrapes and cuts from the scuffle.

During that time in Uganda, kidnapping children for ransom had become almost a fad of sorts. It was all over our local news with new copycat stories almost daily. Very few abductors were ever successful in receiving their ransom and tragically most children, whether their parents handed over the money or not, were found murdered. In order to prevent such an occurrence, all of our children have had their ear pierced. Sometimes children are abducted for child sacrifice and sold for body parts to a witch doctor. For these purposes, a child's body is not to be altered or scarred in any way. A pierced ear is seen by the witch doctor as a deformity. Having to take such measures against such evil is devastating enough, but nothing could have prepared us for an attempted kidnapping for ransom.

Even with the woman's confession, to our disappointment, her time in prison was inadequate. Her brother took it upon himself to punish me for imprisoning his sister. "I know that you are not at home right now, but as soon as you get home, I am going to cut you into pieces with my machete," he bellowed through my phone. How did he get my number? How does he know that I am not at home? I was terrified, racking my brain with questions. Robert called the police and officers were posted around our home, but my sense of safety and security had been robbed.

Things had gone too far and I was ready to admit defeat. Somewhere from deep within I found the courage to stretch my wings and soar above all of this. No one ever said life would be easy, but I knew in my heart that God had not brought me this far to abandon me. In the pain of this terrifying experience, a bright and shining miracle was only two feet away. Isaiah was peacefully sleeping in a small cot next to our bed. He survived and was alive and well – a blessing beyond any measure.

From Carli's Journal

I cannot believe what happened today. I am still shaking. Isaiah was almost kidnapped right from our own compound. He was playing with his brothers and sisters outside and within seconds was in a dangerous stranger's arms. What is wrong with this world? Thankfully our older kids got me from inside before it was too late. I fought for our son. If it had come to it, I would have fought until death. Isaiah is sleeping now but I refuse to leave his side. The reality that he could have been sold for body parts to a witch doctor or held for ransom has hit me hard. I could have lost him forever. Thank you, God, for protecting our son.

Chapter 11

With an ever growing family and rent in town soaring to over one thousand dollars per month, we knew that having a place of our own was vital. We always dreamed of our children having a forever family home and knew we wanted to expand our Abetavu project beyond our walls and into a village. During one of our fundraising trips in Canada, we were blessed with enough financial support to purchase land. Once back in Uganda we were connected with a Canadian man who was working for a very well-known and established faith-based, non-government organization. He specialized in purchasing land for the NGO, so we were encouraged that he would be a great asset in our venture for land.

Buying land is very risky in Uganda because of many false land owners and titles. The chance of purchasing land and soon discovering that you were scammed was extremely high. The people involved were very rarely convicted nor was the money re-reimbursed. With every belief that we had avoided such a mess, we started the hunt for a piece of land that best suited our vision.

Standing in an overgrowth of grass, weeds and acacia trees, it was hard to imagine that this would be our home. I am not too good at visualizing things, but fortunately Robert could see the whole layout before him. He led me around the land showing me where our family home would be, where we would develop a farm for animals and where we would plant and grow food to help sustain our family. Near the proposed site for our family home we would construct a row of satellite houses. These homes would provide emergency shelter for women and their children escaping from abuse and be a stepping-stone into adulthood for our children as they matured past adolescence. Everything had its place.

I climbed to the top of a termite hill hoping to be able to picture his vision, but instead I was chased back down by angry termites. It was not the 'welcome home' I was looking for! This was definitely going to be a new adventure. The air was so clean and revitalizing. The lush green terrain held new life. The soil was so rich it would never refuse to yield a crop to feed our ever expanding family. Yes, this was definitely home, but first the termite hills had to go!

From Carli's Journal 

Today I saw where our future permanent family home will be. Right now the land just looks like a bunch of trees and bush and termite hills. Unfortunately from today's ventures, I have learned that termites have a nasty bite but, that said, the land is still amazing. I am just excited that we are able to make such a big step and purchase land. This is a huge step towards our dream for our family and to be able to help raise up a village.

Our new Canadian friend went ahead and started the process for purchasing the ten acres. When it was time to wire the funds through, he suggested they be directed into his Ugandan female friend's account. We deemed it wasn't necessary because I had my own account in a local bank. He informed us that the land was being sold for $40,000.00 CAD. Once the money came through, we handed it over to him and he informed us that he was going directly to purchase the land from the original owner. After months of pleading, he finally provided us with a legitimate land title document.

In Uganda it is common to find people squatting on your land and it can be very difficult to remove them. We decided to build a structure near the entrance to show that the land was inhabited. The same man that helped us secure our land offered to help us find supplies and construction workers. We handed over another $1,500.00 CAD for this support. After a month we went to check on our land, excited to see the progress. To our dismay, we found a handful of used iron sheets nailed to sticks forming a small metal box. There was not even a door.

The local Chairman of our village area council came by. "Are you the people who purchased this land?" he inquired.

"Yes," my husband responded.

"You must come with me. The original owner has filed a complaint and you are not permitted to erect even one post until this is solved," the Chairman instructed.

Confused, we followed him to his office. He placed what appeared to be legal documents on the table in front of us. In bold block letters the document stated that we were being sued by the original landowner for $2,500.00 CAD. Were our eyes fooling us? How could this be?

"Madam, I am sorry to be speaking poorly of your family, but your father ran away without paying the remaining payment for the land," stated the Chairman.

"My father? You mean the white man who was helping us acquire the land? He is not my father! He was just our land broker. I swear we gave him all the money for the entire land. We handed over $40,000.00 in full," I replied hoping this was just a small misunderstanding.

"Madam? $40,000.00? Are you sure? The land was negotiated for only $15,000.00!" He handed us the official agreement of sale.

Robert and I stared at each other in complete disbelief. My heart beat rapidly with intense anger. How selfish and heartless could one person be? Hiding behind the walls of the NGO he claimed to be a man of God. Yet he had devised such an evil plan. He knew how we struggled to raise the funds for the land and how people had worked hard and so graciously donated their money. Most importantly, the land was for a children's home! Children who were once orphaned and abandoned. Children who more than anyone deserved this opportunity to have a forever place to call home. He had met our children and had even kicked a soccer ball around with them. Yet the whole time he was busy conniving and scamming together with our lawyer! Only God knows how the money was divided, but they got away with an outrageous total of $25,000.00. Our lawyer had likely made two documents every time a signature was needed. The only difference between the two legal documents was the price of the land.

Immediately we went to the person who had referred us to their 'trusted employee'. We explained every detail, but the man did not seem to show any bit of the shock that was shaking our bodies. "Carli, I was hoping that this would not be the case. We have just discovered that he has been behaving in the same type of manner with our NGO. He has been let go. His termination will be published in this week's newspaper. I am so sorry. I had no idea it would end up like this." His eyes were now swollen with tears.

From Carli's Journal

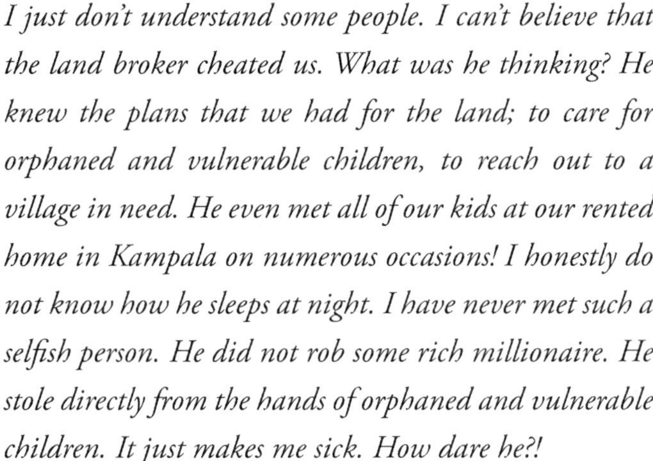

I just don't understand some people. I can't believe that the land broker cheated us. What was he thinking? He knew the plans that we had for the land; to care for orphaned and vulnerable children, to reach out to a village in need. He even met all of our kids at our rented home in Kampala on numerous occasions! I honestly do not know how he sleeps at night. I have never met such a selfish person. He did not rob some rich millionaire. He stole directly from the hands of orphaned and vulnerable children. It just makes me sick. How dare he?!

Since this was not the land broker's 'first rodeo' as they say, he left little evidence to prove his actions. I tried to call him, but his phone was switched off. We met with the land owner and paid the remaining $2,500.00. If this balance had been paid, we may never have discovered that we had been scammed.

I often wonder why he left the balance. Was he so consumed with greed that he faulted in his game plan? Ugandans often say, "God made man. Man made money. Money made man mad." This saying surely fits this case. Later, this man started his own Ugandan charity and for some obscure reason he used me as a character reference! I was contacted through e-mail when one of his donors was very concerned about the use of his funds. I shared my experiences and soon it was discovered that he had continued his scams to the point of trafficking children in the business of illegal adoptions. I do not know whether he is hiding out in Uganda or Canada. He may even be in the middle of another scam. Life eventually catches up with all of us. One day, one time he is going to be held accountable for his actions. It may be in front of man or maybe even God. If I were him, I would hope to be reprimanded by man.

Even though we had been betrayed, we thanked God that we finally had the Land Title in our hands. I refused to let this obstacle discourage the plans for our children, our family and the village that would one day be our home. It seems obstacles were becoming a regular occurrence, but instead of accepting defeat, I was learning to fly over them.

Chapter 12

I was disappearing, shrinking underneath my clothes. Everyone saw it but me. "Sweetheart, please, you need to eat something. You are becoming a skeleton," my husband would plead. I was living in the city with almost any food that I fancied at my fingertips although I had absolutely no desire to eat. Three days could easily go by without me realizing that I had not even eaten a single thing. I completely lacked the sensation of hunger. Robert was busy preparing our land in the village and unless someone sat in front of me with a spoon to my mouth, things were only going to get worse. In one month we were going to travel to Canada. Unfortunately, I came down with malaria. I had encountered malaria several times, but this was the first time I was hospitalized and put on an intravenous drip. A week after I was discharged, I was in a car accident and cracked two of my ribs and received a nasty gash on my head. In the midst of all of the chaos, I was numb. It was as if I was emotionally switched off from the world.

When most people are having a hard time, they tend to turn to food for comfort. I, on the other hand, completely shut out food. My body adapts, I lose my appetite, and when forced to eat, I find it a huge challenge and can be quite irritable. Something was resonating from deep within me. The control that I had over my body, even if I was hurting myself, felt empowering. Without meaning to, I was going into a downward spiral of lies.

From Carli's Journal

I don't know what is wrong with me. I cannot eat if my life depended on it. I am not starving myself so that I can be a supermodel; it has nothing to do with the way I look. It feels so much deeper but I just cannot put my finger on it. I feel like I am fighting a battle within myself, but I don't know why. Food has become my enemy. Robert keeps fighting with me to eat but merely bringing the fork up to my mouth seems like an impossible task. I know that I cannot continue starving my body like this but I also don't have any urge to fight the problem. Everyone says that I am wasting away but I just don't see it. My clothes are definitely too big for me but I still feel like everyone is over-exaggerating. I will be fine.

The last time that I had been in Canada I was a healthy 125 pound woman standing at 5'9". Now as I stepped off the plane in Canada, I was a dangerous 105 pounds. Astonishingly, I was immediately craving my homeland fix of 'two cheeseburgers, fries and a root beer.' However, this time

I did not 'scarf' it down. After nibbling on a couple of fries, I decided to finish once we reached my parents' home. It was a standoff between me and the two burgers and the burgers seemed to be winning. Just from the smell I could literally taste the sugary ketchup and the melted cheese on the thin patty, but the act of actually lifting the burger to my mouth and taking a bite seemed impossible. "Carli, eat your food. I thought this was your favorite," Mom pleaded.

"It is, but I can't. I want to, but I just don't know," I tried to explain.

"Just eat," Mom replied with deep concern. I wished it was that simple. I had a serious problem and it could not be ignored. I needed help.

Days later, I met with a beautiful wise woman. She understood the depths of my pain. Speaking honestly and kindly, she helped me to discover that my eating disorder was derived from my intense need for control. During the sexual abuse that I endured, I had lost all control. Now, years later after the abuse, I was subconsciously obsessed with the need to have control and starving was my vice. There was a huge inner battle going on, and because I was still not confident enough to take back control over the abuse that I faced, it instead had led me down another deceptive path. My eyes filled with tears and burned with anger. I just wanted to be free. The sexual abuse robbed me of my childhood innocence and stole my dignity and self-respect. My abuser left scars so deep that, even more than 10 years later, I still could not shake them. The wounds were still surfacing, but I'd had enough. "God please, I can no longer be a captive to my abusers painful grip. Please save the terrified little girl inside of me and set my feet on a firm foundation as a strong woman. I want to fly free without fear. From this day forward I want to live my life as a survivor," I prayed with a hopeful heart. Filled with a sense of peace, I set my feet on the ground and kept moving forward.

From Carli's Journal

This is becoming too much for me. Why does he still have such control over me? When will I ever break free from the grasp of his perverted actions? Now because of him I was going to starve myself to death all because I am so very desperate to have some control over my life. He is a very controlling man so it makes sense that it has all come down to this. God please help me! Give me the courage to stand up for myself, to break free, and to fly above the pain.

This was not going to be easy, but it was a necessary part of my personal healing journey. I would love to say that my appetite magically came back. Even though I had discovered the source of my eating disorder, it had already become a bad habit. I yearned to take back control over my life. Eating continued to be a challenge when I faced an emotionally draining or stressful time, and unfortunately this is common in our daily life. I still struggled with the belief that my abuser was the winner. He had been given a 'Get Out of Jail Free' card and escaped the confines of prison. Even if I had the courage to take a firm stand against him, the guilt that he brainwashed me with as a child clouded my mind. As much as it disgusts me to admit, he had gotten into my head so deeply that I felt sorry for him.

If I did take this stand it would mean that I would finally be able to cut him out of my life. I wanted no more e-mails, family get-togethers or painful encounters, but whenever I got this far I would talk myself out of it. What if my extended family hated me for it? He already has a bad heart. What if he has a heart attack and dies from the shock of my stance? As much as he had hurt me, I never wished death upon him. I only regret that he never faced any legal repercussions. I really wanted to break free but his grip and the guilt was intense. I could not understand why I even cared what the outcome would be or how I could have any concern over the feelings of my abuser. Never one to want to 'rock the boat,' I was drowning at his luxury. I hated myself for it. That day was not the day that I would finally say 'Enough is enough,' but with the sun shining brightly over the horizon, I remembered God's promise that I would be free and soar like an eagle. It was time to start stretching my wings. When I was ready, freedom would be mine for the taking and what a day that would be!

Chapter 13

My time in Canada was over. Returning back home to our children after traveling is often bittersweet. They are filled with joy and excitement, but we are exhausted and jet-lagged. Of course, we are ecstatic to be back home all united again, but when your beautiful children have prepared a day's worth of songs and drama and your eyelids are weighed down heavier than a ton of bricks, it can be quite overwhelming! Once rested, my heart began to fill with joy. Lying in bed hearing our children laughing and playing, I soaked in the rich aroma of chicken soup cooking over the charcoal stove. Amidst the scampering of little bare feet running in and out of the house, I sensed someone was missing. I needed a hug from one more precious daughter, and then I would truly be 'home sweet home.'

While I was in Canada, our youngest daughter's biological family had come to our Ugandan home and had taken her back to their village for the Christmas holiday. It was not uncommon for one of our children to go and visit a family member that we had deemed safe and responsible. In fact, we encouraged it.

"Hi, how are you? When will you be sending back our little angel? We miss her terribly," I rambled into my phone and eagerly waited for a response.

"We have decided as a family that she needs to be with her blood relatives. Her father wants her back. She doesn't need you anymore," her Auntie stated sternly back through the phone.

"Doesn't need me anymore? But I am her mother. Please don't do this," I cried falling to my knees on the cement floor.

Flashbacks of memories of this daughter filled my head. She was my first baby. She made me a mother. She toddled into my life off the street at the tender age of one and was now being ripped out of my life only months before her seventh birthday. How could this be? I could not breathe. I was gasping for air. My daughter! I wanted my daughter, but how could I even begin the process of getting her back when I was too distraught to even crawl out of my home?

From Carli's Journal

Today was a bittersweet family reunion. Without our youngest daughter, my precious angel, nothing felt right. I called her Auntie but to my surprise she was quite harsh and said that I would never see my daughter again. I am speechless! I am terrified! I am distraught! It is hard to even breathe. I cannot even fathom how I will live my life without her. I refuse to even accept such an atrocity. I must get her back!

With the encouragement of my husband and visiting cousin, I was able to divert my pain into a fierce determination to get our little girl back. Armed with a letter from our Child Protection Officers that stated by law the child must be returned into our care, we started the eight hour drive to our daughter's village. The van could not move fast enough. Once we reached our destination, even though exhausted, we headed straight for the local Child Protection Office. Equipped with all the necessary documents, we confidently walked into the office. The person in charge was on our side and wrote an official letter requesting the head police officer to escort us and place our daughter back into our care. I was glowing with excitement. The next morning I would be holding our daughter and had no plans of ever letting her go.

"Yes. Okay. If you can provide the transport, we can go. What these people did was not right. This must be handled as a case of kidnapping. This is very serious," the police officer in charge grunted as his eyes peered over his newspaper. After his necessary cup of 'chai,' we were finally en route. It seemed like every herd of cattle was sent to block our path. Even chickens joined in, but nothing was going to keep me from our daughter. As we entered the gates, I quickly scanned the compound but she was not there. We were invited into the home, but only her biological father and aunt entered the room. I had no time to waste in the traditional Ugandan greetings. Instead I demanded to see our daughter. This was not the time for polite welcomes because clearly I was not fine.

"Where is she?" I demanded.

"She is at school," the aunt replied.

"At school? But it's the weekend. How could this be?" I rattled back quickly, desperate to locate our daughter.

"I put her in boarding school," she jeered back.

This was all too much for me. Boarding school? But why? She was only six years old. The main reason the aunt claimed that she was taking our daughter was because she needed to be with her blood relatives, yet instead she had put her away into a boarding school. I was infuriated. Anyway, none of this mattered. I had come to get our daughter, not to fight with these people. It was simple. We could just go and pick her up from the boarding school. The aunt started hurling insults at us, so I told the police officer that we should go.

When we entered the car the police officer's demeanor changed. "I cannot help you with this case. Your child's aunt is a very powerful person in this village. She is the women's leader and is very well connected. If I help you, I risk losing my job. I think that you should drop the case," he insisted.

I could not believe my ears. This was not happening! I have

dealt with corruption but not of this level. "Please Sir, I cannot lose my daughter. They don't even want her. They are just playing games. Please, there has to be something you can do," I pleaded as tears welled up in my eyes.

"Go to Family Court and see if they will receive the case," he suggested. Well then, Family Court was where we would go. The case was accepted by the judge, letters of invitation were given to the concerned parties, and the proceedings were to be held the next morning.

> *From Carli's Journal*
>
> *God please, I am on my knees begging with every part of me. Please reunite us with our daughter. You are the one that brought her into our life in the first place. Please do not take her away like this. Please hear this Mommy's cry.*

I did not sleep the whole night. With my trusty cousin by my side, I headed to the courthouse. As soon as we arrived, it was clear that corruption had full control. Our daughter's aunt, the infamous women's leader, was busy laughing and flirting with the all-male jury. She even managed to have a quick moment with the judge. The courthouse was packed. We may have been the first white people to have had a case there, and it appeared that the whole village had come to witness this rare event.

First, the aunt gave her side of the story. She repeated the importance of the child being with blood relatives and stated that she was willing to cover any expenses related to the care of the child. Like her puppet, the biological father claimed how we would sometimes refuse him to enter our home and see his daughter. While talking, he never took his eyes off the aunt's. Her mouth silently prompted his words. It was clear that they had rehearsed. Then, it was my turn.

I knew in my heart that the jurors' and judge's decisions had already been made. I still wanted them to hear my story, the truth, so that when the time came they would have to hold the fate of my daughter in their hearts. That is, if they even had hearts.

"Our daughter was thrown away, abandoned. She has been in our care from the time she was an infant. In the past six years, her aunt only visited her once when she was two years old. Her biological father has a serious drinking problem. He is rarely employed and instead spends his time in the bar. On several occasions he has come to visit his daughter when he was severely intoxicated and behaving badly. We did not find it appropriate for him to visit when he was in that condition. Let us most importantly think about what is best for the child. I clearly did not produce her, but I love her as my own. She is my own. She needs to be back with us, her family. If these people wanted her so badly, then why did they throw her away like a piece of garbage? They claim that blood relatives must be brought together, yet the child, at the tender age of six, has been put into a boarding school. Please, choose wisely for the sake of the child," I pleaded. My heart was pounding. My words were all that I could offer. The decision was out of my hands. My cousin also spoke out with words of support, but as with me, her words also fell on deaf ears.

"Madam Carli. We can see that you really love the child, but is it not possible for you to put your love on the shelf? When she is 18 years old she will come and find you if she chooses. Just put your love on the shelf until then," the judge suggested as if he had given the perfect solution. He was clearly not on my side.

"Your Honour, for many reasons you clearly do not have or understand the heart of a mother. One cannot possibly put their love on a shelf," I replied as my final plea to get our daughter back.

"It is time for the jury to help us reach a decision. Gentlemen, please advise us. Should the child be returned to her biological family? Please stand and comment," the judge summoned. Six men rose in front of me. I felt as if I was about to be sentenced to death. One by one the cowardly men declared a simple "Yes." Not even one made eye contact with me. As the fifth man said "Yes," we stood up and backed out of the court room.

"You are all corrupt and I hope that God punishes you," I

shouted when I neared the exit just as the final man stated "Yes."

"Madam Carli, please come back," the judge shouted over all of the commotion. It did not matter. With 6 yeses and an equally corrupt judge, the verdict was obvious. My cousin and I escaped into an empty courtroom. The reality of my daughter being taken away from me hit me hard and I collapsed down into an empty bench. I sobbed and sobbed and sobbed. When I opened my eyes, I was surrounded by women from the village. Our words may have been lost in translation, but as mothers they wept with me and for me. In all my despair this was my hug from heaven. When I got the strength to stand, my cousin and I left the courthouse to look for our hired car.

The aunt, the women's leader, the supposed Christian mentor, was blocking the gate with the jurors. They were all sneering and snickering as if they were 10 year old bullies waiting for me on the school playground. We continued walking and as we passed through the evil crowd, the verbal attack began. "Your family is bull shit. You look like bull shit. You are bull shit," the aunt spat, her face ugly and construed. It was quite the public statement coming from the village's respectable, godly leader.

I could have fired back a hateful response. I could have physically taken her down, but that is what she wanted.

She was egging me on, trying to make me snap, so I fought back with the only option that can infuriate such a person. My weapon of choice was silence. I walked past her to the waiting car and never looked back. Miraculously, I was able to hold back my tears until our car drove away. The aunt was left bewildered and appeared foolish in front of her so-called friends and followers.

From Carli's Journal

Today was one of the hardest days of my life. The court refused to give us back our daughter. I did not even get to see her sweet face as she is locked away in a boarding school. I did not get to console her, to reassure her of how much we love her. I do not want her to grow up thinking that she did something wrong or that we did not want her anymore. It makes me sick to think about the lies that her family must have filled her head with about us. I agree that it's in the children's best interest to be with their biological family, but that is only when they are safe people that can provide a nurturing environment, not people just playing games at a child's expense because they are concerned with how things look at face value. If they really wanted to bring her back into their family with the right intentions then this could have been handled in a much different way that would have been way less traumatic for our daughter. As hard as this is

> *for us, this whole situation is way more detrimental for our daughter. I can only hope and pray that God will put someone in her life that will show her the love and care that she deserves. I am so thankful for the abundant words of encouragement and prayers that our friends and family from Canada and the 'Facebook' world provide. We were never alone in any of this. I am not angry at God for not giving our daughter back, but I would be lying if I said that I am not confused by the outcome. I am grieving the loss of her daily presence in our life. As hard as this is I truly believe that we have not lost her forever.*

We learned that after our daughter's first term in boarding school, her aunt stopped paying her school fees. Sadly, she has not been able to settle into any family but keeps being passed around to different relatives who likely treat her as a burden. This is not the life that our precious daughter should be living. Since the court made its decision, all I can do is pray for her safety and protection.

"My dear daughter, I think of you often. You are deeply wanted and loved as an important member of our family for life. I still grieve the loss of your presence, but I have a real peace that one day you will walk back through our door."

Chapter 14

The time had come for the big move to the Abetavu village. Robert had spent the year chasing away angry machete wielding villagers who kept fighting over our land. He left every morning at 7:00 am to see the project site of our new home and came home in the evening battling traffic at 8:00 pm, repeating this day after day for an entire 10 month time period. He sacrificed many precious moments with our family so that our home could be constructed with less hiccups. Even if he had missed one day, bags of cement would have magically gotten legs and walked away.

Heavily pregnant with our fourth child, I took advantage of my nesting urge and started packing up a household of 20 people and 20 peoples' things without the convenience of cardboard boxes. I had to be really creative in my packing arrangements, using basins and even pillow cases to store things. Then, three weeks after a caesarean delivery of a healthy baby boy, we were in a procession of white pickup trucks to our forever family home. We led the way in our seven passenger van packed with 12 children, six dogs and a cat. It was pitch black when we arrived. There was no running water and the power had gone out. None of the beds were assembled.

We connected mattresses in one room and tried to convince the young ones that it was fun, just like camping. We were all exhausted, but it was still hard to fall asleep in the unfamiliar environment.

"I want to go home," Isaiah started to cry.

I had to stop myself from joining in with his tears. I was excited for our new home, but change has always been hard for me. Taking in a deep breath, I knew that I had to suck it up and lead by example.

"We are home Isaiah. In the morning when the sun comes up, you will see how great everything is," I said as I gently stroked his cheek. I am not sure if I was trying to convince my son or myself. It seemed that we both needed a pep talk.

The sunrise was spectacular. Opening the door of the balcony was like opening heaven's gates. Everything was going to be fine. As soon as we stepped out the door we were surrounded by new faces. I was the only *mzungu* (white person) for miles. Adults were confused by me, children were enthralled by me, and babies were terrified of me. I could never go far without finding a trail of children in hot pursuit, taking turns to quickly touch and poke my oddly coloured skin. My tattoos did not help either. The children laughed about how such a big person could draw on herself and they rubbed my skin hard to see if the tattoos would come off. It was definitely a new but good experience.

Our older kids were thriving. This is the life that they had always dreamed of with fresh air, endless space to run in, trees for climbing and an abundant supply of fresh fruit. They felt at home the second that their feet hit the ground.

Living in the city for so long had spoiled me. I had been too lazy to learn much Luganda as it was not necessary in Kampala. In this village though, Luganda was a must unless all I ever wanted to communicate with my neighbours was a polite "How are you?" I went from having every convenience and shopping amenity at my fingertips, even delivery, to a fruit and vegetable stand down the road. Realistically, I probably should have mentally prepared myself for my new village life, but with a new baby and the anticipation of the move, I had not even considered how settling in would be. However, I learned that upon hearing that a *mzungu* woman was coming to live in their village, the men had bet on whether I was going to last or not. Unsurprisingly, their odds were not in my favor of ever settling in. Never one to want to be proven inept, I used their lack of faith in me to fuel my fire.

Maybe this was where I would find freedom. Physically, there was more than enough room to start stretching out my wings. With my new found determination, I was mentally ready as well. Freedom was at my fingertips. It was mine for the taking. It was time to fly.

From Carli's Journal

We are living in our new, beautiful, family home. It is ours. No more landlords. No more rent. No more packing. No more moving. No more unpacking. No more changing the kids' schools. We are settled once and for all. This new life in the village will take some time for me to get used to, but not in a bad way. I just need to learn the ropes of village life and get a better grasp of the local language, but it is all worth it. Our family is so blessed beyond measure!

Chapter 15

It was our regular bi-weekly excursion to Kampala. Village life had won me over quicker than I had imagined. The dusty chaotic roads in the city were now overwhelming. Activities moved at a hectic yet unpredictable pace, leaving me stressed and at times even gasping for air from all the pressure. With our closest bank branch in the main city, we had no choice but to brave the journey, leaving the tranquility of the village behind. As usual, I found a long queue at the bank. I never understood why there were six slots for tellers but I never found more than two staff behind the plexiglas stalls. After what seemed like an eternity, I finally reached the counter. I withdrew a large sum as we still needed to pay some of the builders and complete the remaining projects for our extensive home.

With my handbag secured firmly under my arm, I walked out of the door and into the parking lot. There were many more vehicles than parking stalls, so I ventured into the maze of metallic barricades doing my best to squeeze between any openings that I could find. I found Robert doing his best to settle a very hungry baby Zion in our van.

"I am so sorry! As usual, the bank was packed," I explained as I quickly gave baby Zion my breast. Robert skillfully reversed into a sea of madness. Before pulling out, our side door was yanked open and someone jumped in. I was busy feeding my hungry little one, so I just assumed it was Robert's friends catching a lift. An unusual silence filled the air. As I turned my head to peek a glance at the mysterious passenger, my head was immediately shoved forward by the barrel of a handgun.

"I want money from bank," he yelled, pressing the gun firmly into the back of my neck. Beads of sweat ran down my face.

"Please don't hurt us! Take the money!" I pleaded.

"First, he drive far!" he ordered.

"Man, just take the money," Robert urged.

"Drive!" he shouted back, digging the barrel of the gun into my husband's shoulder. "Drive or you die," he continued to repeat as we ventured on a road unknown to us.

My heart was pounding and every inch of my body was trembling. My biggest fear was falling into place as we were led to a deserted compound. This man wanted more than our money. He also wanted me. "Get out. Give me money now! Now!" he shouted. As I handed over the package of money he grabbed my wrist tightly. "Catch baby and don't move!"

he yelled at my husband.

"Please! Kill me but leave my wife!" Robert pleaded.

But the man had already made up his mind. He threw me to the ground and tears silently rolled down my face. The barrel of the gun was pressed firmly against my temple. I closed my eyes and prayed. He forced himself on me for what seemed like a lifetime but only minutes had passed. His friend came and they drove away.

They had spoken many words to us, but I heard nothing.

I was screaming, but no one could hear me. The sound radiated throughout my entire being, but not even a murmur left my lips.

Robert lovingly carried my limp body to the van. Silence consumed the drive home. I quarreled with God as I collapsed on my bed. How could He let this happen while I was still struggling to work through my abusive past?

From Carli's Journal

Today felt like a nightmare. I wish that was all it was. We could have died today but God spared our lives. This was not our time to go and I am so thankful for this. I have spent the whole day crying and now I feel numb but the most important thing is that I still have my life to even feel these emotions. I see life a lot differently today. Absolutely every moment in life is precious. I hope to never take anything or anyone for granted again. Tonight I am going to hug everyone a little harder and a little longer.

Through the love and prayers from some very special people, I felt a warm presence of peace. My husband, baby Zion and I had our lives spared. I learned to rejoice in this. I also knew deep down that God had not abandoned me in my time of despair. He had never left me in the past and never would in times to come. We live in a world where evil is ever-present. God did not turn a blind eye on me. He wept for me. My pain was His pain. The burden was not mine to carry. I was not going through this alone. God had placed angels on earth just for me and brought them into my life in miraculous ways.

The little girl inside me was still begging to be freed from the chains of abuse. With her fists clenched, banging against the walls of my inner core, she was not going to give up. I knew she was right.

I knew in my heart that I would soon taste freedom as sweet as honey, but I was also terrified. The time to be free was inching closer, but unfortunately that day was not the day. Falling to my knees I cried, "God, please give me the courage to help myself. I am scared."

Chapter 16

The act of helping people is not as glamourous or as easy as most people believe it to be. It is actually easier to do more harm than good. As the saying goes, "Give a man a fish and you feed him for a day. Teach a man to fish and you feed him for a lifetime." If all that I have done is teach my village to be dependent on me, then I have truly failed. This has become my daily struggle.

"Madam, come quickly!" a neighbour came pleading, gasping for air. What I found was horrifying. It was as if the family home had been attacked by rebels. Pots and torn bits of clothing were scattered on the dry red earth. Dark smoke billowed from the thatched roof of the mud hut.

"What has happened?" I asked the man who had brought me.

"That man there! This is his family home. He said that he had quarreled with the wife over money and sent her back to her mother's home with their five children. Then, when he came back from the gardens, thieves attacked him and burnt his home," he explained.

"I am not the police. Why did you bring me? How can I help?" I questioned.

"Madam, something does not add up," he replied. He was right. The man of the house was heavily intoxicated. Nothing appeared to be stolen. Instead it looked like the aftermath of a serious fight. A nauseating smell that I had never experienced before was coming from the hut. My heart ached as I walked toward the hut.

"Take down the door," I ordered, my voice shaking. With one swift kick it was down. The putrid smell of burning flesh engulfed my entire being. Precious, lifeless bodies were huddled in the corner. The mother's body was draped over her little children protectively. The urge to vomit got the best of me as I fell to my knees. "Put the fire out!" I ordered the stunned onlookers.

The police were called and the bodies were carried out one by one. Under the heap of bodies, a baby, an angel, lay completely unscathed, as if she was just sleeping. I picked her up and gently stroked her cheek. Choking on my tears, I walked towards the man of the house with his lifeless child gently cradled in my arms.

"Do you see what you have done? Does this make you a man?" I screamed, extending my arms with his dead child towards him. "You evil man! You murdered your wife and five children! For what? For what?" I demanded.

"She refused to give me money for drink!" he exclaimed drunkenly as he staggered away from me.

I sank down onto a wobbly wooden bench clutching death itself in my arms. My head hung low and my shoulders slouched with the weight of the world.

Since a man in the village had burned his entire family alive, word travelled quickly. Women were wailing and throwing themselves onto the ground and an angry group of men wielding stones and large sticks had formed. The police finally arrived and threw the man into the back of a white pickup truck. With mob justice a common solution for thieves and murderers, he is lucky that he escaped with his life.

It was decided that a group burial would be held the next day. Measuring the baby and the children's dead bodies for the appropriately sized casket and then shopping for them was one of the saddest things that I have ever had to do. Caskets that small should never even exist! Placing the bodies one by one inside the wooden frames, I also placed a charm bracelet with a bird and a heart pendant on each of their wrists. This was to signify that they were all loved and now free from the trauma and pain that had been inflicted upon them.

I closed the mother's casket last. "I am so sorry. Sorry that you and your precious children were taken like this. I don't understand any of this but you will be my driving force for change in this village. You were an amazing mother, so brave. I am so, so sorry," I wept, too distraught to leave her side.

From Carli's Journal

I don't even know where to start. What I have seen today is still so raw in my mind that I don't even know how to grasp it. A beautiful mother and her five precious children were brutally murdered by a man that was supposed to protect and care for them. Each of their lifeless bodies is engraved in my heart. I cannot get the images out of my mind. When I try to lie down and close my eyes I see them. I tried to have a nap and I dreamt of their hut burning down and I could hear their agonizing cries for help. I woke up in tears and I have not been able to settle since. The terror. The pain. I cannot even imagine it. This is a family that used to dig on our land and now they are gone. There is no way that I will be able to sleep tonight.

Morning came too quickly. It seemed as if the whole village had come. "Madam, we were unable to locate any relatives. We are requesting that you lead the burial," the village Chairman requested.

"It is fine," I replied with no truth in my words. It was time to open in prayer. With swollen, red tearful eyes, I poured out my heart to a somber crowd through the translator.

"My dear friends, this tragedy could have and should have

been avoided. Precious, precious lives were lost right here in our village. It's all because a man who was supposed to be trusted as a husband and father was denied money to go and drink. We must come together for the sake of our children. Please turn to the people next to you, look them in the eye and tell them, 'Never again.' Tell them, 'Never again.' We must learn from this and move forward from this," I preached, praying that I had been heard. "Please, never again," I sobbed as I dropped to my knees in front of an ever-growing crowd. Life in the village would never be the same after this. The death of this mother and her children would not be forgotten.

From Carli's Journal 

Today was the burial. I was asked to lead the proceedings. It was all so surreal. I did my best to keep strong and not break down, but at certain times my emotions got the best of me and could not be controlled. I begged and pleaded with the large crowd that had gathered that this should never, ever happen again. I can only hope and pray that my plea did not fall on deaf ears. As the coffins were lowered one by one into the ground, a part of me wanted to jump in after them. This last event in the funeral was too final for me. I was not ready. With the coffins being covered in soil and people leaving back to their homes, I had to face the full truth that this really did happen, that these precious lives were so selfishly taken. As nightfall comes, I am still not ready to accept that. Only time can heal such pain.

Due to this one mother's bravery to cover her children with her body as her final efforts to save them, numerous outreach programmes have been initiated in her honour. She inspired us to start a teen girl's support group, a football club, a children's church, a community library, community gardens, a school sponsorship program, a mobile children's clinic, parenting workshops, a daycare program for children with special needs, vulnerable children's home visits, girl's sexual abuse and rape advocates and so much more.

With help from numerous supporters we are able to help thousands of people in our village and the surrounding villages. This is not a 9 to 5 job. There is no leaving unfinished work on the desk at the end of the day before going home. We are in the depths of our family and community life on a 24 hour daily basis. We are not afraid to get our hands dirty and live every second of every day with no regrets. I could not imagine my life any other way. I am in my element, and even in the hard times, I thank God for putting me exactly where I am. Through my husband and our family and the beautifully vibrant people of our village, I am blessed beyond measure.

My life is at risk sometimes for standing up for those who

are not given a voice. I refuse to keep silent. Tragic cases involving children and women in our village are brought to my attention daily. Getting involved often means having to confront men with respected leadership roles or religious titles. Challenging them is deemed inappropriate, especially by a woman. I do not value the title if the person is abusing his or her power. I firmly believe that justice for the victim needs to be achieved no matter who is involved. My stubbornness has created some enemies for me. Sadly, I am rarely able to attain adequate justice for the victims, but big steps are still taken when their voice has been heard. Self-empowerment is priceless and many have gone on to encourage others to break the silence of their suffering.

Some tragedies are still being brought to my attention when it is too late to intervene. Recently, in only the span of one year, I have buried seven more children all under the tender age of six. Instead of the families coming to ask for help for urgent medical treatment for their child, they come and ask for money to buy a coffin and to pay for transporting the body to the burial site. I continue to plead at children's burials for the parents to take preventative action. All I can do is hope that my plea does not fall on deaf ears. No matter how many times I have buried a child, nothing can ever prepare me for such sadness and sorrow. My heart of a mother still carries a dull ache from all of the loss.

My dear angels fly high and free. You will never be forgotten.

Chapter 17

The year of 2014 was full of hope and promises. I was 10 weeks pregnant with our fifth biological child and excited for what was to come. I wanted to wait for the traditional three months to pass before sharing the news and I am thankful that I did. "Robert, I am bleeding. Please come quickly!" I cried into my phone. It was all happening so suddenly. No cramping, no pain. There were no warning signs at all.

Lying on the bed I wondered how this could be. I pleaded to God to save my child but after having a scan, I surrendered. Helpless. I lost my baby. A feeling of emptiness took over me.

"You will need a D&C first thing in the morning as things are not progressing naturally," the doctor told me. I was admitted for the night with the intention of starting the procedure early in the morning. Because of a disagreement between doctors over when to start, the procedure was delayed. I was wheeled on a gurney to the operating theatre. I was left alone for three hours and was forced to listen to women going in for a caesarean and hearing their baby's loud cry coming into the world. I hated feeling so angry, but being forced to share their joyous occasion was pure torture. My husband was so loving and encouraging to me, but I could see that inside he was also distraught.

When I reached home that evening, I slowly entered the kitchen. Our son Akiz came running up to me and placed his hands on my abdomen. "Mommy, you had a baby girl in your tummy, but don't be sad. She is in heaven now with Jesus," he said with such warm assurance. I gently smiled down at him and then went upstairs to rest. No one back at home knew about my pregnancy and the loss. They thought that I had been in the hospital receiving treatment for malaria. God had used my precious four year old son to give me a comforting embrace straight from heaven. Everything was going to be okay.

From Carli's Journal

I never knew that a miscarriage could leave such a feeling of emptiness in my life. The pain of losing a child in the womb is like no other. It is not the physical pain but the emotional pain that broke me. I had life in me and then, just like that, it was gone. I was put on the labour ward for the D&C. Hearing women shouting in labour and then their babies crying its way into the world felt like a cruel punishment while I waited for my procedure to take place. I just wanted to get it over with as soon as possible and go back home. Minutes felt like hours. I wanted to run away, but I knew that I had to first face what was ahead of me. Robert was so kind and compassionate throughout it all, but the pain in his eyes was too much for me to bear at times. He did his best to keep strong but his eyes spoke the truth. Like me, he was also devastated. We just got home and our son Akiz told me not to worry, that my baby girl is now in heaven with Jesus. I am completely caught off guard by this. Thank you God, for using our son to bring comfort to our broken hearts.

It was time to push forward. In all my 29 years, I had never fully learned how to drive a car. With Robert's amazing support, I was off on an adventure. I did my best to avoid pot holes and maneuvered around chickens, goats, cows, and small children. I am so proud of myself for this accomplishment. It really got me thinking about what else I could do to improve my life.

After deep reflection I knew what I had to do. I dusted off a beautifully bound journal that I had been keeping for such a moment as this and I began to pour my heart out onto its crisp, white pages. I wrote every day, not stopping until my hand would go numb. My pain saturated the pages, forming words to describe the burdensome memories that I had carried for far too long. I was on an emotional roller coaster ride, but the rawness was freeing. This was my story to tell and finally I was back on my journey to healing and freedom.

Writing down my story helped me to see that I, Carli Travers, was the one holding myself back and now 'Enough is enough.' I needed to free myself from my abusive past. Letting myself get eaten alive by a burden that was no longer mine to carry had become a relentless affliction of self-torture. My health was deteriorating and my eating disorder was quite serious at times. Overcome by a multitude of emotions, I had literally reached the monumental make or break moment of my life. If I wanted to continue being a dependable wife, mother and friend, I needed to believe in more for myself or I would never be good for anyone. I could not keep teasing myself with just the mere taste of freedom.

I deserve it.

I want it.

God wants it for me.

A big part of my healing is forgiving my abuser.

It is one of the hardest choices that I have ever had to make. Forgiving him does not excuse his behaviours nor release him from the responsibility of his actions. Instead, it gives me the opportunity to let go and have peace. I have to accept the fact the he may never admit publicly to his actions. I may never receive a genuine apology, but that is his burden to carry now and not mine to bear. It has always been about control for me, but forgiving my abuser does not mean that he has won and I have been defeated. It means that I have released the chains of abuse that have consumed me for far too long. I have allowed myself to start the journey to recovery that I finally believe that I deserve. Forgiving acknowledges the pain that I endured at his hands. There will be no phone call, letter or e-mail to the man that robbed me of my childhood innocence. I will not initiate a face-to-face reconciliation. This is what I need to do, what is best for me and what I am comfortable with so that I can truly be free and heal from the deep wounds of abuse.

I need to have an intimate talk with the little girl within me in the safety and security of God's presence; acknowledging the pain that she endured, directing the blame to the abuser, and praying from deep within my heart for forgiveness towards the man that inflicted the pain.

The time has come to set her free from the prison cage that she had been locked in for far too long.

I am nearing the eve of my 30th birthday.

Again, I am brought back to the scared little girl inside of me. I reach my hand towards her and pull her into the safety of my arms. "We are OK now. He can never touch us again. He can no longer confuse us with deception and lies. We are in control now. We have no guilt. The abuser no longer has any right to be part of our life. I have forgiven him but that does not excuse his despicable actions."

"Look how far we have come! God never abandoned us and He wants to take away all our fears, hurt and pain. He wants us to be free and that starts with you. It is time for us to say goodbye. Be brave and proud.

The silence has been broken. Our story has been told. At times it has been painful to tell, but it has been an important part in our journey to freedom. We did it! We really did it! Beautiful girl, do not dwell on the pain and hurt anymore. Stretch out your God given wings. Fly high! Fly strong and never look back!" I calmly cooed to my inner self.

Gently releasing herself from my embrace, she smiled and my heart smiled back.

She spread her wings, blew me a goodbye kiss and soared away high above the clouds with great ease.

Her laughter echoed from the heavens.

Her joy radiated down to the earth.

And then she was free.

PRAYER FOR FREEDOM

Dear God,

You alone know the depths of my heart.

You know every detail of the pain that I suffered.

You know my deepest, darkest secrets.

I ask that you bring to the surface what needs to be healed and set me free from the abuse that I endured.

I want to be free from my painful past and move forward to the future that you have in store for me.

Please give me the courage to overcome and persevere.

Make me whole again.

Give me strength and bring me peace.

In Jesus' name,

Amen.

And then
She was Free

^ Carli aged 9 months

v Christmas morning. Carli aged 13 and sister Kristin aged 7

Carli and Robert aged 22. Climbing the hills of Robert's village in Kabale with his Uncle Bahat (2007)

Family picture at the source of the Nile. Back row, left to right, Carli, Robert, Tina, Martin, Middle row: Marjorie, Godance carrying baby Isaiah, Vanessa, Douglas, Benjamin, front row: Julianna (2008)

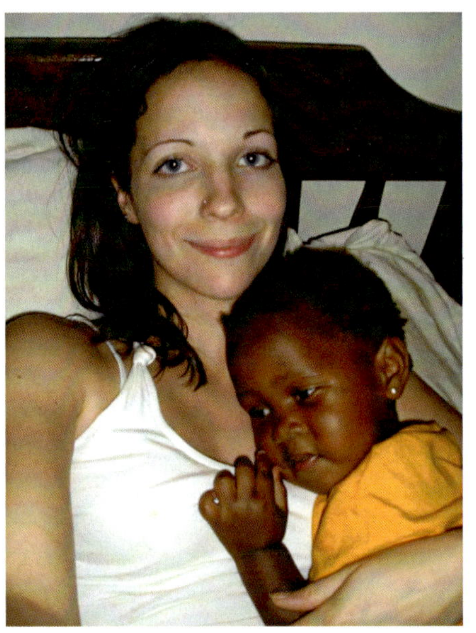

^ The original 6. Tina, Carli & Julianna, Godance, Vanessa, Martin and Benjamin (2007)

< Carli snuggling with her precious daughter Julianna (2007)

< Carli and Daniella in the community library. Daniella died suddenly only 2 weeks after this picture was taken (2014)

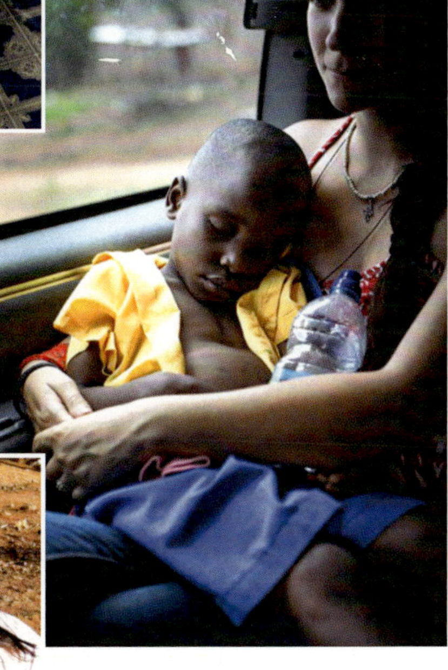

> Carli bringing home Colin to join his forever family (2014)

< The outreach picture is me at the Gayaza Market (2013)

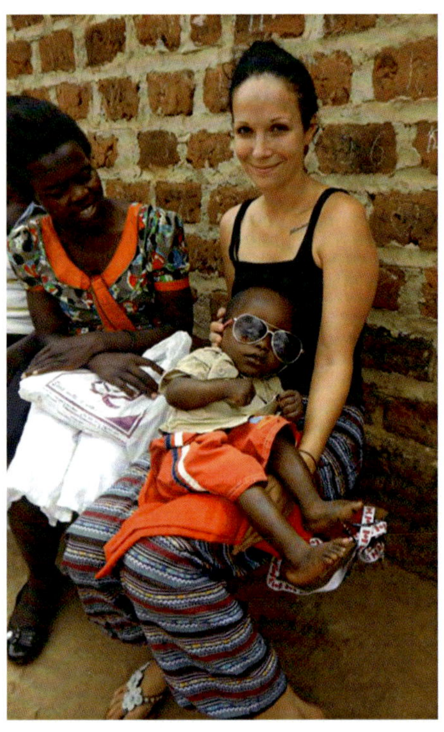

< Carli on a home visit with her staff member Barbra to Edrine's home to check on his health. He was born with severe disabilities (2014)

v Robert cutting the cake at a Christmas outreach party for the children in the village (2012)

^ Robert and Carli's son Zion hanging out with his best buddy Michelle at their children with Special Needs Day program (2015)

v Isaiah, Akiz, Codrine, Colin and Xavia taking their sister Justina our for an evening stroll (2014)

The magnificent 10 acres of land that houses the Abetavu Family

The ever expanding family Back row, left to right:Annette, Sandra, Deus, Robert, Carli, Elijah, Martin, Benjamin, Douglas, Middle row: Christine & baby Jeremiah, Mukaka, Godance & Justina, Tina, Front row: Xavia, Isaiah, Codrine, Zion, Akiz, Colin and Yawe (2014)

About Abetavu

Abetavu (Safe Haven) exists to provide hope for a brighter future for Uganda's vulnerable children and Women. It was founded in the mid 1990s, by Canadian native Carli Travers and her Ugandan husband, Robert Birungi.

They have dedicated their lives to raising abandoned children in a nurturing, family setting. They have just added a 20th child to their family and are constantly in need of funds in order to bring in more children on a regular basis.

In the past 2 years, Carli and Robert have extended far past their family responsibilities and the borders of their land. They have initiated a Primary School Sponsorship program that sends over 200 children to school, run a daily Soccer Outreach program for children, youth and young adults, lead an Adult Literacy program, run a Teen Girls group, have a community library, advocate for women and children at risk, provide emergency shelter for women and their children that are escaping from abuse. They also recently started a Day Care program for children with Special Needs and a Parent

Support group as their major activities. In effect, they are creating an integrated community with a common goal: to create an environment where children and their families will learn to strive for a brighter future.

If you would like to make a financial donation or learn more please visit our website at **www.abetavu.com**

To order additional copies of

And then She was Free

Please visit our website at

www.abetavu.com